SLAVES OF OUR GODS

To Diane Hovey
Best Wishes
James Bupp

JAMES R. BUPP PHD

ISBN: 1503125033
ISBN 13: 9781503125032
Library of Congress Control Number: 2014919988
CreateSpace Independent Publishing Platform
North Charleston, South Carolina

CONTENTS

CONTENTS BY LIFE LESSONS

We grow old too soon and too late smart! - An Old Dutch saying.

Lesson Twelve: There are old pilots and there are bold pilots, but there are no old bold pilots. - page 38

PREFACE

I DEDICATE THIS writing to my wife, Jeanette V. Bupp. Sometimes she patiently waited for me to complete this book, and at other times she asked, "Why is it taking you so long?"

She frequently asked if she is "in the book," and I finally told her that I would give her an "honorable mention." And so, my dear Jeanette, you have brought a whole new dimension into my life in the last twenty years, and it is with love and gratitude that I officially honorably mention you, Jeanette V. Bupp, as my number-one supporter and mentor in all of my writing efforts. Thank you, Jeanette.

INTRODUCTION

It has been more than five years since I published my first book, *The Last of the Family Farms,* available on Amazon). In that book, I recounted what it was like to have grown up on a family farm some sixty years ago. I attempted to write about my early childhood and my learning experiences so that my children and my grandchildren might really know something about me and about the lifestyle our family shared as we made our living on the Bupp family farm.

I marketed my book on the Internet and at Wegmans Food Market in Canandaigua, New York (a second- and third-generation family-owned grocery store started in Rochester by John Wegman in 1915) where I worked part-time. It was through my work experience at Wegmans and the book signings that I gave at Wegmans, libraries, service organizations, and historical societies that I began to receive some feedback from the people who bought my book and had some understanding of a lifestyle rooted in agriculture. This feedback ranged from "You mean you actually cut off the chicken's head? That's disgusting!" to what more than a few of the menfolk said to me: "I could have written that book if I had just taken the time to write down my own childhood experiences." (It was a bit humbling to learn sixty years later that many others had shared my early experiences of growing up in an agricultural society and that I wasn't as unique as I had previously thought!) Most people today know nothing about the work involved in raising animals and vegetables for food, and their knowledge of food is limited to what has been served to them in a school cafeteria, sold to them at the local grocery store, prepared at home, or purchased in a restaurant.

But I also met people who were either from my generation or who still enjoy an agricultural lifestyle and understand firsthand what is involved in raising your own animals and vegetables—not only for food but to make a living. Sadly, those who are involved in making a living by agriculture today are in a very small minority—less than 2 percent of the US workforce is employed in agriculture as of year 2000. (United States Department of Agriculture, "The 20th Century Transformation of U.S. Agriculture and Farm Policy", Carolyn Dimitri, Anne Effland, and Neilson Conklin) http://www.ilovefarmers.org/downloads/The20thCenturyTransformationof U.S.AgricultureandFarmPolicy.pdf

My part-time job at Wegmans enabled me to meet and talk with all kinds of people from various walks of life. And in the course of performing my daily tasks of greeting customers, handing out food samples, and helping customers find various items in the store, I learned a lot about people, their expectations, their concerns, and their frustrations. I observed and spoke to many parents and grandparents, and they like me were somewhat bewildered by what is going on in our society. They sensed that the changes we are experiencing today have put us on a track that is causing a lot of social, economic, and political conflict. Living in this society is a lot more disruptive and less satisfying than it used to be. Indeed our current lifestyles seem counterproductive to making a living, raising children, and really getting to know our families, friends, and neighbors.

In this book, I go back to the place where I started and attempt to deal with the question of why our society has changed so much in the last fifty years. Perhaps by reliving my own journey, I'll discover some answers about what has caused all of these changes, and then, armed with this knowledge, I might be able to better understand what is happening in our society today and perhaps get a glimpse of the future.

1

LEAVING THE AGRICULTURAL SOCIETY

MY OBJECTIVES WERE quite fuzzy when I left home at the age of eighteen to attend college. What was clear to me was that my oldest brother had been chosen to inherit the family farm and that my mother wanted me to attend the same college that she attended when she left her family home near Smithville, Ohio. She had graduated from Manchester College in North Manchester, Indiana, in 1933 with a Bachelor of Arts degree in biological science. (Manchester College is a liberal arts college affiliated with the Church of the Brethren, the same church my mother attended all of her life.) She also thought that I should become a preacher, but her wishes just didn't seem to fit into the direction that I wanted to go in life.

In the late fifties, electronics played only a very small role in our lives. You have to remember that television came into our homes only around 1950. I loved to experiment with magnets, generators, and batteries, though. Much to my father's disapproval, I disassembled an old crank phone that we had in the attic for the magnets that were inside. In my freshman year in high school, I built a Heathkit ham radio transmitter, and I obtained my Novice license. In those days, a Novice license restricted one to using Morse code unless one had the resources to buy phone radio equipment, which I didn't. But one huge event occurred in 1957 (my junior year in high school) that changed everything: the Soviet Union launched their Sputnik satellite. Suddenly, our country woke up and recognized that we needed engineers and scientists to develop our own satellites and satellite-launching capability. And in our little rural community of Smithville, Ohio, it became "socially acceptable" to become an engineer and to seriously study science. Before Sputnik, acceptable careers for students were farming, teaching, preaching, automotive repair, journalism, and homemaking. But with the launch of Sputnik came a broadened acceptance of science and engineering as legitimate career choices. The attitude and curriculum of the local high schools didn't change overnight, but I was encouraged enough to start thinking about a career in science. I also have to note that from an educational point of view, I was ill prepared to enter into a scientific career. My math skills were woefully lacking. No trigonometry or calculus courses were taught at Smithville High School, just two years of algebra. But the wonderful thing about being young is that all that seems to matter is the destination. Preparation for a long journey into the field of science was something that could be accomplished along the way.

2

My Learning Journey

AND SO MY journey began as a hopeful science major at a liberal arts college. I would regard my first year as one of survival and adjustment to dormitory life as well as to being away from home for the first time (other than a couple of one-week stays at a summer church camp). My parents gave me enough money to pay for my tuition and my meals. The freshmen were assigned seats in the dining room for lunch and dinner, which were served family-style. Table assignments lasted for six weeks, and then one was assigned to a new table so that in principle, one was able to meet all the members of the freshman class in a year. Toward the end of my freshman year, I began to wonder why I was never assigned to a table with some of the better -looking women. I found out later that the seating assignments were fixed, but I never did find out who did the assigning. (Lesson One: Rules are made for someone else's advantage—even at church colleges.) Breakfasts were more to my liking, because they were served in the cafeteria and we had some choice in what time to go and what to order. My first class (French) was at 7:30 a.m., so I didn't have much choice about when I went to breakfast: 7:00 a.m.! But that was approximately the time that we had breakfast on our family farm, so I was used to early morning hours. Wednesday mornings were an exception in that there were no classes until 10:30 a.m. All students and faculty (about 1,100 people) were required to attended chapel in the auditorium at 9:00 a.m. for announcements, hymn singing, and a short service. Most of the students relished Wednesday mornings because they could sleep in for a couple of extra hours. The administration discouraged us from missing chapel on Wednesday mornings by adding to the number of hours required for graduation. If you had more than three absences in a school year, additional course hours were added to your graduation requirement. I once calculated that if you chose not to attend Wednesday's chapel at all, it would take you more than seventeen years to graduate!

Manchester College had a lot of rules in those days that would definitely be regarded as old-fashioned by most and more likely barbaric by today's social standards: the women were locked up in their dormitories (there were two women's dormitories when I attended) at 10:00 p.m. on weekdays and Sunday evenings, but on Friday and Saturday evenings, the doors were kept open for another hour, until 11:00 p.m. In addition, a female student was granted two extra hours of evening freedom on either a Friday or a Saturday night. That meant she might stay out until 1:00 a.m. on one weekend night, but for the other weekend night, she had to be in the dorm at 11:00 p.m. Or she might choose to stay out till midnight on both Friday and Saturday night. The men had no such rules, but we still suffered—probably more than the women!

Other social rules had to be followed as well. Manchester College did not permit dancing on campus, nor could freshmen have a car on the campus unless they were commuters. (Commuters were issued a special sticker for their cars). I would estimate that approximately 70 percent of the students were from communities close enough for them to be able to return to their homes on weekends and see their friends. The campus became a "ghost town" on weekends, deserted by most, and I was stuck in the middle of nowhere without a car. My freshman roommate, Ron Rodkey, was a weekend commuter. He would leave for home on Friday night to see his girlfriend and not return until late Sunday evening. I hated weekends! Yes, there was a student center called The Oaks where students could watch TV or buy an ice-cream bar or a soda, but it too closed at 10:00 p.m. The Oaks had once been an army barrack. It smelled, and the floors creaked of old age. On weekdays, my roommate and I would go there to buy some popcorn and a quart of cooking oil so we could make popcorn in the dormitory during the week to kill our hunger pains. (Cooking in the dormitory was strictly prohibited, but as I recall, my roommate and I bought more than twenty-nine quarts of cooking oil that first year!)

The routine of going to breakfast at 7:00 a.m., classes at 7:30 a.m., dinner at 6:00 p.m., and then studying in your dormitory room till bedtime seemed to drag on and on, especially in the wintertime. But finally the first real spring evening would come—you know the kind of evening I am talking about, when it was still light after dinner, the evening air was damp but warm, and the peepers were singing their song in the woods. It was on such an evening that studying didn't even enter one's mind, and the students would stay outside of their dormitories after dinner just talking and hanging around, enjoying the break in the weather. Such evenings were ideal for the annual spring "panty raid" on one of the women's dormitories. Late in the evening, the men would gather behind the women's dormitory and start singing lovely songs such as "I Love You Truly" or "Goodnight, Irene," but eventually the songs degenerated into "Sheik of Araby (Without No Pants On)." The women would open their windows and throw some "unmentionables" down to the waiting men as a little "thank-you" for the serenade. And then, a side door would open and the men would storm into the dormitory searching the rooms for their own souvenirs. Of course, the dorm mother would go nuts, and after all the men were "chased" from the dormitory, the campus would eventually quiet down in the early morning hours in time for the next day's classes to begin all over again. (Lesson Two: Men do strange things when they are lonely.)

I can hear some of you asking, "Why didn't you pick up your cell phone and call home if you were so lonely?" Well, cell phones hadn't been invented yet, and as best as I can remember, there was only one pay phone in the dormitory where I lived. On top of that, I had no extra money for making long-distance calls. The only connection to my family back home was via letters that my mother would write to me when she had time or the occasional ride home with friends who lived near the family farm some 225 miles away during Thanksgiving, Christmas, and Easter recesses. Somehow I survived that first year, although to this day, I don't know if I was in college, in prison, or in an asylum. As I look back, I think it was probably a combination of all of the above!

My sophomore year went a little better for me. My parents gave me the old family sedan, a 1953 Plymouth, to drive to college. I had learned to drive in that vehicle, but it was well worn out by the time I got it. In those days, salt took a terrible toll on cars, and I can remember being able to see the road through the floorboard as I looked down from the front seat. During one of my college breaks, I patched up the hole with a piece of galvanized metal flashing, some sheet-metal screws, and a little roofing cement that I found in the barn. But I had a car, and it freed me from being a "campus captive." I did very little driving that year other than to return home on school breaks, but nevertheless, just having a car changed my feelings of being trapped while I attended college.

I took my first physics course in my freshman year. It was a struggle, as my math skills were woefully lacking, and I had to scramble to learn trigonometry just so I could do the simple mechanical physics problems. My first physics professor was Dr. Charles Morris, a rather soft-spoken, aging man who had made a name for himself at the college by teaching his courses from his bed while recovering from a heart attack. This was groundbreaking, as it was long before the days of video or telecommunication as we understand them now, and heart attack victims were left to recover in long prescribed stays in bed. He taught his students by using a PA system wired between his home and the classroom as he lay in his bed.

Dr. Morris's interest was in astronomy, and he allowed some of his physics students to help him make the props he required for his astronomy courses. He had some connections with Dr. Charles Stevens, a scientist who worked at Argonne National Laboratory in Joliet, Illinois. Argonne was operated by the University of Chicago and the Atomic Energy Commission. It was at the University of Chicago that the first nuclear reactor was built and successfully tested. The laboratory developed the first marine nuclear reactor for the submarine *Nautilus*. I thought it rather strange that Dr. Morris would go out of his way to buy and deliver half an Indiana beef cow to Dr. Stevens each summer, but I later learned that he recommended and placed several of his top physics students with Dr. Stevens as summer student aides at Argonne National Laboratory. Dr. Stevens operated the world's largest mass spectrometer at that time and did research on carbon dating of rocks and minerals, among other things. He was unique in that he was almost blind and could just read his watch by pressing its crystal to his eye. His neighbors thought he was a little strange because he built his own house on weekends, often working in the darkness of night, sawing boards and hammering nails without the benefit of any artificial light. Dr. Stevens had a great sense of humor despite his physical handicap. His associates would say, "If Charlie can't see it, it's probably not worth seeing."

In the summer of my junior year, I started working as a student aide at Argonne National Laboratory, thanks to Dr. Morris, starting on a path that would lead to my career. (Lesson Three: It isn't always what you know but whom you know that counts.)

The old science building at Manchester College was near the heating plant, which supplied steam heat for all the campus buildings. The science building was just a one-story block building that smelled of the chemicals that were stored there. Coal was brought to the power plant on a spur rail line from the local railroad. One of my friends made a little extra money by helping to unload the flatbed cars of coal into the storage bins at the power plant. When he was on duty at the power plant, part of his job at night was to shut off a steam valve located in the basement of the Administration building. The Administration building housed not only the Administration offices but also the cafeteria in the basement of the building. A women's dorm was located on the second and third floor of the Administration building. On more than one occasion, several pieces of pie would turn up missing from the cafeteria. Those pieces of pie sure tasted good, and my sincere compliments to the ladies who baked them!

All of my math and physics classes were in the new science building that had just opened in 1959. It was a modern, well-lighted brick building that contained the classrooms for physics, math, and chemistry classes as well as the labs that went along with them. There was also a small machine shop in this building that Dr. Morris used to construct his wire models of the solar system and to support the experiments for the physics labs.

The head of the physics department was Dr. L. Dwight Farringer, the head of the math department was John K. Baumgart, and the head of the chemistry department was Dr. Harry K. Weimer. It was through the teaching efforts of these gentlemen that I learned the fundamentals of science. All of them were very dedicated to teaching.

Mr. Baumgart was a very soft-spoken man who had previously served in the air force. At one point in his career, he had been stationed at Thule, Greenland. He had a lot of spare time on his hands there, and he thought it would be a good opportunity to continue his studies towards his PhD in mathematics. Half of the year was mostly dark and 40 degrees below zero, so there would be no distractions from outside activities. But he soon discovered that it was all too easy to just go to a movie or to do nothing, and he lost his incentive to work at furthering his education. (Lesson Four: Nothing is accomplished in this world without some struggle or irritation.) Mr. Baumgart's favorite dessert was ice-cream pie, and the college cafeteria would make it for him on special occasions.

While in his class one day, everyone was struggling with the concept of applying integral calculus to calculate the area under a curve. One of the students raised his hand and asked, "Is there any practical application for this?" "What do you mean by practical?" Mr. Baumgart asked. Can you make a living with the knowledge of integral calculus?" the student asked. Mr. Baumgart replied, "Yes – I am!" Everyone laughed. He was very patient and took the time to explain the theory of what he was teaching and its application. And under his teaching, math became my second major.

My chemistry teacher was Dr. Harry Weimer. He was a rather jovial man and smiled a lot, giving one the impression that he enjoyed his job. He would set up experiments on the lecture table in front of the class to illustrate particular points. One day he demonstrated how to take some magnesium metal shavings and set them on fire, showing us that metals can indeed burn when they are heated to a high enough temperature. The magnesium shavings burned with a bright light, giving off a lot of fiery sparks and smoke. He then took a three-foot-long magnesium rod that was about one inch in diameter and placed one end under a Bunsen burner. He went on to give his forty-five-minute lecture on how metals conduct heat while the rest of us nervously scanned the room to find the nearest exit in case the need arose, hoping and praying the lecture would end soon. Someone asked him if the magnesium rod ever caught on fire, to which he replied, "It hasn't yet!"

Dr. L. Dwight Farringer was the head of the physics department and was a most knowledgeable professor. He had graduated with a bachelor of divinity degree from Bethany Biblical Seminary, and I thought at the time it was rather a strange combination of career paths. Thermodynamics was a course that I struggled with mightily, and I believe I either repeated it or audited it a second time before I completely understood what was being taught. (Lesson Five: The Fourth Law of Thermodynamics: Mother Nature is not the lady she pretends to be!) The extra time and effort that I put into thermodynamics was well spent: I later took a thermodynamics course at The Ohio State University and breezed right through it, whereas many of the five-year engineering students failed it.

Data processing was rather simple in those days. Before 1960, the science departments at Manchester College shared a Marchant mechanical calculator. It was a mechanical marvel that one could use to add and subtract numbers. After entering the numbers into the machine on a keyboard and pulling the handle, the results were printed out onto a roll of paper perhaps two or three inches wide. In my second year I bought a slide rule, which I used to solve many of the math and physics problems. As I recall, it cost around twenty-six dollars, which was a significant amount of money in those days. A slide rule is accurate to three significant figures, and since we were being taught the principles of science, three significant figures were quite adequate. The slide rule is really a marvelous tool that you could use to multiply and divide numbers, look up logs and exponentials of numbers, and calculate trigonometric functions of angles. I used that slide rule not only during my college years but also during my graduate school years. Around 1960, the math department at Manchester College purchased a Fridan calculator, which cost five thousand dollars at the time. For comparison purposes, the price of a new car in those days was about four thousand dollars. One could add, subtract, multiply, and divide on this machine, which was a little larger than a typewriter but was all electronic. The readout was electrically displayed on Nixie (Numeric Indicator eXperimental) tubes, which glowed with small bright orange dots that made up the numbers. One could even do square roots on this machine if one used the mathematical process of iterating to find the square root of a number, but there was no "square root key." But what about computers you ask? Computers were unknown to me and to Manchester College in 1960.

I stayed in North Manchester, Indiana, during the summer of 1960 to take some required classes so I could graduate in four years with dual majors in physics and math. At the end of the summer session I offered to take Dianna Reidenbach to her home in Ashland, Ohio which was on the way to my home near Wooster, Ohio. She was a freshman who had just started working on a two-year secretarial degree. We were to be married in the newly constructed chapel on the Manchester College campus on September 9, 1962, two years after we met.

3

My Introduction to the Atomic Age

After completion of junior year at Manchester College in 1961 and also after graduating in 1962, I worked as a student aide at Argonne National Laboratories in Joliet, Illinois. My appointment as well as several others from Manchester College (including Roger Dillon and Dave Ober) happened in part because of the relationship that Dr. Charles Morris had established with Dr. Charles Stevens at the laboratory, and because we had demonstrated an interest in physics and done well in our studies. In the summer of 1962, we were joined by Ron Brandenburg and Roger Werking, fellow physics students at Manchester College.

Argonne National Laboratory is one of our nation's leading laboratories, operated by the University of Chicago and funded by the US government. It sits on a sprawling site of about four thousand acres, and, at the time I worked there, employed about four thousand workers or about one worker per acre—a figure I have always remembered, since it is roughly the space required to pasture one cow. The world's first atomic reactor was developed and tested at the University of Chicago in a laboratory under the old football stadium in 1940, the year I was born.

And in the ensuing years, the US government funded all kinds of atomic energy research at the Joliet site.

We started our first summer by renting a hotel room in Naperville, Illinois. I remember that the hotel was next to a stop on a major commuter rail line that ran to downtown Chicago. Beginning very early in the morning, the trains ferried people to work and then brought them back home in the evening. After about two weeks of being awakened around 5:00 a.m. each morning by the first train, we moved to Naperville College, a college located at Naperville, Illinois. The college rented out their dormitory rooms for the summer after the school year was finished. For the rest of the summer, we slept in one of the college's dormitories and commuted by car each day to Joliet to work at Argonne National Laboratory. During my second summer at the laboratory, we found a home to rent in Downers Grove, Illinois. The home was owned by a schoolteacher who moved his family into a cottage during the summer, and we truly enjoyed all the comforts of a real home. Four of us from Manchester College lived in Downers Grove while we worked at Argonne National Laboratory during the summer of 1962: Dave Ober, Ron Brandenburg, Roger Werking, and I.

I did not work directly for Dr. Stevens, but my job was in one of the chemistry labs he supervised. It was the responsibility of this lab to do routine mass spectrometry analysis of uranium fuel rods during the enrichment process to determine the ratio of U235/U238. A small amount of a fuel rod was etched away by using acid to dissolve the rod, and then a droplet of the liquid was transferred by a pipette and deposited onto a filament. The water was dried by passing a little current through the filament. The filament assembly was then inserted into the mass spectrometer. After pumping the air out of the machine, the sample was heated by passing a higher electric current through the filament which drove molecules of U235/U234 from the hot filament. The different atomic masses of uranium were separated by a magnetic field. By varying the magnetic field, the two different isotopes would pass by a slit detector and the resulting output from the detector was recorded on a paper chart. The ratio of the heights of the two peaks recorded on the paper was proportional to the ratio of the two isotopes in the sample. A report was then submitted to the requesting lab. My first job was to fill the low-temperature vacuum pumps with liquid nitrogen and to pack the pump's dewars with dry ice for the weekend. Very low levels of vacuum are required for a mass spectrometer to give an accurate reading. An oil vacuum pump cannot be used because the hydrocarbons would contaminate the system and one would observe a peak at each mass number. To achieve the necessary low vacuum levels, both a mechanical pump and a cryogenic pump are required. The liquid nitrogen and the dry ice were stored in another building at the complex, and it was on these daily trips to refill the dewars with liquid nitrogen or dry ice on Fridays for the weekends that I began to explore and to learn what was going on at this vast laboratory site.

Most of the personnel at Argonne National Laboratory were issued special clothing and shoes. You changed into them when you came to work in the morning and then left them at the lab when you changed back into your "street clothing" at the end of the day. The issued uniforms for the men were plain gray work shirts and gray work pants with button flies. The women wore a white "nurse's" type of uniform with buttons down the front. Another curious thing that I observed was that a lot of the workers carried identical gray metal lunch boxes (the old-fashioned kind with the rounded tops and two metal latches on the side) to work each morning. We soon found out what the gray metal lunch boxes were used for, and they weren't for lunch! All of the workers were required to submit a monthly urine sample so that their urine could be monitored for radioactivity. The lab-issued clothing was usually well worn and patched, and the pants often had buttons missing from the fly. You could return issued pants for another pair, but often the second issued pair of pants weren't in much better shape. During the summer months, the men would take their "grays" home on the weekend to do all kinds of mechanical work on their cars, such as changing the oil, or to mow their yards, and then return the soiled uniforms on Monday morning for clean ones. I noticed that some of the men in our group, along with our group leader Dr. Stevens, were not required to wear issued clothing. I asked why only some people were required to wear work uniforms while others wore suits and ties. I was told that if you were on "staff," which meant that you had either a master's or doctoral degree, you were exempt from wearing the rather mundane issued work clothing. And so I came to the brilliant conclusion that I should continue on in my studies for an advanced degree in physics, because I clearly didn't want to dress like that for the rest of my working life. (Lesson Six: Major life decisions are made without having all the facts. If you did have all the facts, they wouldn't be called major life decisions.)

The real reason for the issued clothing at Argonne National Laboratory didn't become clear to me until a little later in the summer. One afternoon I heard a muffled explosion in one of the neighboring chemical labs. This lab was working with radioactive sodium samples, which were disposed of in a stainless-steel DAW (dry active waste) can. Apparently too many samples had accumulated in the can, and when the sodium combined with the moist air, it exploded. That evening, all workers in the affected area were required to have their shoes checked for radioactivity, because the contamination from the explosion had been spread by people walking down the hallway past the affected lab. A young male lab worker who worked in our mass spectrometry lab never wore the issued clothes or shoes because he found them much too plain and uncomfortable for his liking. That night when they tested his shoes, they found that they were radioactive, so they confiscated his shoes, taped up his feet with masking tape, and sent him home sans shoes. This fellow worker was a Catholic, and he would tell me about going to parties where everyone would undress in a dark room, men on one side and women on the other. Then they would head across the room, bumping into members of the opposite sex in the dark! Since I was attending a very conservative church-affiliated college, I asked him about having premarital sex (something that was definitely forbidden in the Church of the Brethren) and what one said to the priest at confession after such parties. He replied, "Oh, I just tell him [the priest] that I was drunk and couldn't help myself." Very creative!

The chemistry labs where I worked were separated from one another by a large grassy lawn. The labs were laid out like the fingers on your hand, with a single hallway running down the center of each "finger." Each of the fingers was connected to the others by a larger hallway at one end that was used as a common service hallway for all the labs in that building. I thought it was a nice design touch that each lab had an abundance of windows with some green space outside for viewing until someone explained to me that the labs were designed so that if there was an explosion in one lab, the windows would just blow out into the grassy way and not impact the adjacent labs. Unfortunately, a fire did break out in one of the labs in the chemistry building during the evening shift, and it was an ugly mess. But as per design, the fire was contained to a single lab.

Dr. Lee Harkness was the head of our mass spectrometry laboratory group and had just completed a documentary film for Argonne National Laboratory about a new robotic arm. The robotic arm could be used to handle all kinds of radioactive materials by keeping the operator of the arm and the radioactive materials separated by a distance or by using some type of radiation shielding between the operator and the material. What was unique about this robotic arm was that it was the world's first all-electronic arm and that the material and the operator could be separated by five feet, fifty feet, or even five hundred miles, for that matter, because there were no mechanical connections between the arm and the operator. Lee demonstrated the arm's dexterity by opening a box of safety matches, taking out a single match, closing the box, and then striking the match on the side of the box to light it. I was allowed to operate the arm briefly. You placed your hand into an "operator arm" that was in the operator's room. The robotic arm followed the movements of your arm: moving your arm forward moved the robotic arm forward, twisting your wrist made the robotic arm twist its wrist, and so on. Pinching your thumb and forefinger together made the robot's "fingers" open and close. One could accomplish delicate jobs like opening a box of matches, or do some heavy lifting by selecting a power switch that increased the operator's strength by twenty-five times. The arm was strong enough to pick up and move forty-pound lead bricks! Our world today is filled with robots that assemble our cars or transport parts through assembly lines, working in conditions that are not suitable for humans. The robotic arm that was all electrically controlled by a remote human arm was invented more than fifty years ago at Argonne National Laboratory and was used to protect humans from dangerous radioactive materials. As you will see in a later chapter, a man's arm and his brains, which operated this first all-electronic robotic arm, are being replaced with a programmed silicon chip!

During my second summer at Argonne National Laboratory, I would frequently visit Building 300, a chemistry building that was under construction. This building was designed to handle experiments with highly radioactive materials. I watched the progress of the construction all summer. The radioactive material was to be stored in lead-lined concrete vaults under the floor of the building. The material housed in these vaults was transported in lead-lined containers to the areas where the experiments were to be performed via a robotic train that ran on tracks along the floor of the building. There was a centrally located roundtable so that the robotic train (a single car) could pick up the radioactive materials and then be rotated in various directions to carry its load of radioactive material to the designated experimental area. The experimental areas were like narrow concrete corridors that extended off from the main floor. At the end of each corridor, was a "window" perhaps two to three feet thick, built from two heavy glass plates. The space between the two glass plates was filled with a radiation-absorbing liquid. Building 300 was at least two or three floors in height off the ground. The most dangerous radioactive experiments were conducted on the ground floor, whereas those experiments that used materials of lower radioactivity were conducted on the upper floors. Consequently, the walls of concrete were thickest at the bottom, perhaps two to three feet thick, but thinner on the second and third floors. The summer came to an end and I never did see the completion of this building, nor did I get to see the robotic train in action, but I can imagine that the experiments that were done in that building greatly contributed to our Cold War efforts against the Soviet Union.

4

PUFF, THE MAGIC DRAGON

THE TIME BETWEEN my leaving Argonne National Laboratory at the end of August 1962 and my starting graduate school at The Ohio State University in Columbus at the end of September is only a blur to me. I married Dianna M. Reidenbach on September 9, 1962, at the little chapel on the campus of Manchester College. After a brief honeymoon in Michigan, we returned to Ashland, Ohio, broke. Our means of support would be my teaching assistantship in the physics department at the university and my wife's job in the foreign students' admissions office.

We hurriedly took a trip to Columbus to find some kind of an apartment. Because school was almost ready to begin, there weren't many choices left in our price range, but we found a place on High Street just across from the university. The apartment was on the second floor of one of the street's older homes that had been converted either to businesses or to apartments for students. The entrance to our building was set back perhaps five feet from the sidewalk along High Street. The door to High Street was locked, but each of the five apartments in the house had a buzzer button at the High Street entrance. If someone came for a visit, they could press the button to your apartment. When the buzzer rang in your apartment, you pressed a button that unlocked the front door to the building. The back of the building had a key-locked entrance and there was a   fire escape which ran from our second floor living room / efficiency kitchen to the back of the building. Our apartment consisted of just two rooms and a bathroom, but it was a start, and we could both walk to the university, which was just across High Street.

There was a dry-cleaning establishment between our apartment building and the sidewalk along High Street (the space that would normally have been the front yard). A hall-way that connected our front door with the apartment building ran alongside the dry-cleaning establishment. The Charbar was next to the dry-cleaning establishment and was well visited by undergraduates, especially on weekends when Ohio State hosted a Big Ten football game at the Riverside Stadium. Football games were big in Columbus, and on football Saturdays the town was flooded with visiting fans from all over the state that brought in a lot of money and excitement. Tickets were in short supply and the games were always sold out, with attendance never falling below the stadium's capacity, which was eighty-three thousand people. Ticket scalpers were to be seen everywhere, offering tickets to the game for thirty-five to fifty-five dollars, which was a lot of money in those days. Married graduate students had the last choice to purchase tickets to the football games and the location of their seats was behind the goalposts, which were ten yards behind the goal line. As I remember, our tickets cost fourteen dollars each for the season, but it provided something for us to look forward to on game weekends, and I dearly loved to watch and listen to the Ohio State Marching Band along with all the color and excitement that goes with Big Ten football. Several years later, we did attend a Cleveland Browns game in Cleveland, but the enthusiasm and color of professional football paled in comparison to the Big Ten football games held in Columbus.

During the 1960s, Woody Hayes was the head coach and the games themselves were rather boring, as his offensive game strategy was "three yards and a cloud of dust." The success of his strategy depended upon the defense holding the opposition's score to no more than one or two touch-downs and perhaps a field goal. But Woody was a legend in Columbus, and each fall he kept the stadium filled with people. And the Ohio State football fans took the games very seriously. One Saturday when Ohio State was losing, an airplane flew over the stadium pulling a banner that read "Goodbye Woody." Such an act was heresy in Columbus, and the outrage was expressed all over the front page of the Columbus newspaper the next day, demanding that the pilot's license be suspended.

On football Saturdays, I would resume my studies in the evening. The Charbar was always busy in the evenings, but on football Saturdays, it was exceptionally busy with students celebrating after the football game and into the wee hours of the morning. The Charbar had a jukebox, and during the sixties, "Puff, the Magic Dragon" by Peter, Paul, and Mary was a huge hit. I would guess that we listened to "Puff, the Magic Dragon" probably more than fifty times on Saturday nights. It's the one song that still remains in my head after all these years, but with a little practice, I was able to tune it out along with most of the other celebrations that occurred in the Charbar next door.

Just behind the Charbar next to our building was a similar apartment building. Usually, there wasn't any noticeable activity in the second-floor apartments behind the Charbar, but on football weekends, the lights would be on in these apartments, giving the impression that they were occupied. One spring night of my first year while I was studying at the kitchen table, there was a knock on the door that opened onto the fire escape. I slowly unbolted the door, and there stood a man carrying a small briefcase. He asked, "Where are the girls?" I replied that only married students lived in this building. "Buddy, you must be in bad shape!" he said, and he turned around and went back down the fire escape. I am sure that he was looking to connect with some of the action above the Charbar and had come to the wrong building. But now that I think about it, his comment was prob-ably correct, although for a couple of different reasons. My first year of graduate studies was tough. Most of my classes contained seventy to eighty students, some of whom were five-year engineering students. I was used to competing in classes with seven to ten physics students at Manchester College, but now the competition was ten times greater. And there was very little opportunity to get much personal help from the professors, because they delivered their lectures and then promptly left the lecture room.

Other challenges also arose during that first year. Ohio's state government found itself in rather bad shape financially, and the governor took it upon himself to solve the fiscal crisis by dismissing all the state employees who had been hired in the previous six months. Dianna was a new state employee at the university, and the loss of her income was devastating. But in just a few short days, the governor discovered that there were no cooks, housekeepers, and other kinds of workers at many of the state institutions and hospitals, and he had to rescind his mandate. My wife was hired back at the university within about two weeks, but she vowed to find another job in the private sector that was not subject to such political whims. Near the end of the school year, she was successful in finding a secretarial job at Industrial Nucleonics, which paid better and was more to her liking. Despite all of the trials and challenges of that first year in graduate school, we managed to survive, and in the spring, we found a nice new apartment just a few blocks north of the university. This apartment had air-conditioning, and I would go there to study for my final exams even before we moved in, as our old apartment was not air-conditioned and became unbearable when it was hot outside.

In my second year, I had to withdraw from a class (Quantum Mechanics) in which I was not doing well, thereby learning yet another important lesson. (Lesson Seven: Failure is a part of the learning process.) And just as the Ohio State football team often did, I had to punt the ball back to the other end of the field and regroup. I rescheduled the class when I had mastered the appropriate mathematical symbolism required to understand the concepts of the course. There were many times when I would get discouraged and think I had done badly on a test, only to discover that most of my classmates had done worse and I would still end up with a good grade. (Lesson Eight: Successfully competing [in a class, in a race, or for a job] doesn't mean that you have to score 100 on every test or break a record in each race. It means that you have to be just a little better than the others in the competition.)

Sometime during my second year at Ohio State, I began looking for an adviser and met Dr. C. V. Heer, a professor in the department of physics. He was working on low-temperature studies as well as on microwave studies, which included research involving masers (microwave amplification by stimulated emission of electromagnetic radiation). Cliff was a very stern man and was not at all interested in taking on graduate students who were interested in obtaining only a master's degree. According to his way of thinking, it was a waste of his time to take on master's degree candidates, so I once again raised my sights to graduate with a doctorate. Dr. Heer had obtained some money from the US Army for a research grant, and at the end of the second year, I was working under his direction as a research assistant. This was much more to my liking: I much preferred working in a lab on new ideas to helping undergraduates with their physics laboratory experiments. Dr. Heer had proposed to build a ring laser (actually it operated in the infrared region of the spectrum) that could possibly detect the rotation of the Earth as measured from some "fixed star." The concept of his proposal was based upon the Michelson-Morley experiment performed a long time ago. In 1887 in what is now a part of Case Western Reserve University in Cleveland, Ohio, Michelson-Morley set out to prove that light traveled through some kind of medium or "luminiferous aether." Depending upon the speed of the aether in relation to the sun, they thought, they should be able to detect a change in the speed of the light, just as one would detect a change in the speed of a mechanically induced wave in water, depending upon the direction in which the water flowed in relation to the observer. But alas, their experiment failed and only proved that regardless of the Earth's position in relation to the sun, they could detect no difference in the speed of the light coming from the sun (within the experimental error of their interferometer setup). With the extreme monochromaticity of the "light" emitted from a laser, Dr. Heer proposed to re-explore the limits of detecting motion by using a rotating laser cavity.

My decision to continue on for a doctoral degree presented its own special hurdles and challenges, which included a residence requirement, the demonstrated ability to read and understand two foreign languages, a dissertation that represented some original research work, and finally a written and oral examination of my knowledge of physics.

One of Ohio State's more famous sons was Jack Nicklaus, who was an undergraduate while I was there during the sixties. He never graduated because he was always playing in some golf tournament in the spring and summer months so he couldn't meet the residency requirements, and the university refused to award him his undergraduate degree. His first major win was the US Open in 1962. We would on occasion drive by Jack Nicklaus's house, which was then in Upper Arlington, but no one was ever there! It was ten years later, in 1972, after Jack Nicklaus became a golfing legend, that The Ohio State University conferred on him an honorary doctorate. In 1984 he was also awarded a Doctor of Laws honorary degree by the University of St Andrews, Scotland. (Lesson Nine: If you don't play by the rules, don't expect to be rewarded.)

The hurdle of demonstrating an ability to read and understand two foreign languages proved to be far more problematic for me. I had already taken two years of French in my undergraduate studies, so after taking two quarters of French at Ohio State, I felt ready to take the exam for my doctorate. I passed that exam fairly easily; it was the German that really gave me trouble. I took German at Ohio State and found myself studying perhaps fifteen hours a day just trying to keep up with the undergraduate course assignments. There was little time left for anything else. To pass the language requirement, I studied German for a full year, an extra workload that added a year to the time I spent at Ohio State (six years in total). The foreign language requirement has since been eliminated for doctoral candidates at Ohio State. (Lesson Ten: Life presents many hurdles and challenges that you have to overcome. Deal with them and move on.)

Most of my course work was completed by the end of the third year, allowing me to spend the majority of my time working in the lab with Dr.

Heer. The laser cavity that I built to detect the rotation of the Earth with respect to some fixed star was in the shape of an equilateral triangle with the laser-amplifying tube positioned along one of the triangle's legs. There would be two infrared beams traveling in opposite directions. A detector was placed on the outside of one of the cavity mirrors, and with the help of another mirror outside the tuned cavity, the two (clockwise and the counterclockwise) beams were combined and a detector measured the resulting signal. As the cavity was rotated, the detector would detect a beat frequency that was proportional to the speed of the rotation. All of the components (with the exception of the aluminized mirrors) were built right there at the university. I learned to do my own glassblowing and to work in the physics shop to make all the necessary hardware required for the experimental setup. According to the theory, the laser cavity should have detected the Earth's rotation even as the apparatus sat motionless on the table, but no motion was detected. We next tried to suspend the entire apparatus—cavity and five-hundred-pound granite table—from a strap secured to the ceiling of the physics lab. With this suspension system, the table could be rotated very smoothly and slowly, and one should have been able to observe beat frequencies proportional to the rotational speed of the rotating apparatus. Still, the Earth's rotation was not detected when the cavity was at rest. Another one of Dr. Heer's students, John Little, demonstrated on an earlier cavity that the speed of the Earth's rotation could be detected, but one had to keep the cavity in constant motion for a given period, counting the total number of beats. The beats were then counted for the same period of time in the reverse direction. The difference between the number of clockwise and counterclockwise beats was caused by the rotation of the Earth. In my experiment, when the rotational speeds became close to the speed of the Earth's rotation, the two beams would "lock" in frequency, and no further angular rotation could be detected. This was very disappointing, because it meant a "no" answer for my experiment! Fortunately, Dr. Heer considered my work good enough and accepted it as my dissertation for the doctoral degree.

There is a huge time lag between the completion of research work in a university and that work being reduced to some practical application or reported in the public news media. When I was in graduate school, we knew that Honeywell was able to actually machine three-ring lasers into a single spherical ball of quartz, but we could not say anything about it. It wasn't until around 1988 that I remembered seeing an article in *Popular Science* that explained how the United States' battleships were able to fire their sixteen-inch guns with projectiles that weighed a ton or more and hit targets some twenty miles away in seas that caused the ship to pitch and roll. The article described how a laser gyro made by Honeywell detected the motion of the ship's gun barrels (with respect to some fixed star). With the help of a computer, the gun was fired at the precise moment when the barrel of the gun was in its proper position to hit the target. To those of you who hunt, target shoot, or shoot skeet and trap, it's known as Kentucky windage when you take into account the distance to the target, the movement of the target, the trajectory of the bullet, and the speed of the wind, and aim accordingly.

I left the typing of my dissertation to my wife, who was by then an experienced secretary at one of the local technical companies. She did all the typing of my dissertation on an IBM key typewriter (IBM had just introduced a new line of electric typewriters called the Selectric in 1968) at her place of work in the evenings and on weekends. Typing a dissertation brings its own special requirements: kind of paper, type size, and so forth. We had to buy a whole set of special technical letters and symbols such as the Greek alphabet and mathematical symbols such as an integral sign to properly type the dissertation. Each symbol or letter was attached to a small handle, which was manually inserted into a modified typewriter. The impression of the special symbol was made by striking any key on the typewriter. Dianna's help was invaluable in producing the final version of my dissertation.

Things began moving at a rapid pace. The final hurdle for me was to pass the general exams and a final oral exam. In the spring of 1968, I spent three months preparing for the general physics exams. I did most of my studying in the physics building at The Ohio State University, and it became like a job to me, going to work in the morning and then coming home in the evening, seven days a week. About two weeks before the final exam, I became mentally and physically exhausted. I couldn't study anymore but felt confident that I was ready to pass the test. I can imagine that athletes arrive at a similar point in their training just before a big race. You train and train, and then you reach a point where you can't do anymore. All of the hard work paid off, because I did pass my general exams and then later passed the oral exam, which I had to take by standing in front of my adviser Dr. Heer and several other professors in the physics department. After the oral exam, they signed my papers and I ran (yes, ran) as fast as I could to the graduate school admissions office to file my papers before any of them changed their minds!

The events of that summer in 1968 just flew by. I accepted a job with the IBM Corporation in Endicott, New York. Dianna was pregnant with our first child, and the baby was due near the first of September. I worked feverishly to finish up all of my schoolwork and to go job hunting in preparation for graduation at the end of the summer quarter. And graduation day finally came in August 1968 when I graduated with my PhD in physics from The Ohio State University. Seven thousand other people graduated on that day. First the undergraduate degrees were conferred en masse, then the master's degrees, and finally the doctoral candidates walked up onto the stage one by one to receive their degrees. It was the proudest moment of my life! We celebrated the event afterward with a little dinner at our apartment with my parents. Two weeks later, on September 6, 1968, our son Michael James Bupp was born in Columbus. Talk about timing! We moved to a duplex in Endicott, New York, and I began my job on September 29, 1968, as a staff engineer at IBM Endicott.

5

MACHINES SHOULD WORK; PEOPLE SHOULD THINK

Neither of the Watsons, Thomas J. Watson Sr. or Thomas J. Watson Jr., uttered these words. Thomas Watson Sr. certainly did utter the word "Think" many times and it was chiseled onto the steps of the development building in Endicott, New York. Thomas Watson Jr. did say in 1957 that "Machines might give us more time to think but will never do our thinking for us." (IBM Archives) I did not use a computer during my undergraduate studies (Manchester College did not have one at that time), nor did I use one during my graduate studies at The Ohio State University. Yes, Ohio State had computers in the sixties, as did many of the large universities and companies that required them to do a large number of repetitive calculations. The computers of the sixties were typically owned by universities, large corporations, banks, or the state and federal governments, and were used to tabulate and compile large databases of information or, in the case of universities, to perform iterative calculations to solve complex mathematical problems. But now I was going to work for IBM, a company whose very name was synonymous with computers!

At the end of September 1968, I drove to Endicott and waited at our duplex on Smith Drive for our furniture and belongings to arrive in the moving van. The moving van arrived on Sunday afternoon, and I started to work as a staff engineer the following Monday morning. Dianna, her mother, and our newborn son, Michael, would arrive in a few weeks by air after I had had a little time to unpack some of our possessions. From this point on, my life was to be forever changed, as now I would make my livelihood in the industrial society. My journey from the agricultural society to the industrial society (from the time that I left the farm until I started work at IBM in Endicott) had taken ten years, and along the way I had become a husband and a father as well as earning my PhD in physics.

IBM Endicott holds special significance in the IBM Corporation, because Endicott was the corporation's birthplace, according to Kevin Maney (2003) in his book *The Maverick and His Machine*. In 1914, a company known as the Computing-Tabulating-Recording-Company, was joined by Thomas Watson Sr. The C-T-R Company sold scales, clocks, and tabulating machines. It was in Endicott, NY that Thomas Watson Sr. headed the company that he renamed International Business Machines or IBM.

I never knew or met the Watsons. The statement "That there would only ever be a market for five computers" was generally attributed to Thomas Watson Sr. in the late forties. But in his book, *The Maverick and His Machine,* Kevin Maney could find nothing written down that connected Watson to this statement. It was really Tom Watson Jr. who championed the new electronic age that began to unfold in the fifties and sixties. While I worked at IBM (1968–1998), corporate IBM became much divided about the market that IBM should serve in regard to computers. The large mainframe computers were a salesman's dream, and the top salesmen often met their yearly sales quotas in the first three months of the year! In the seventies and eighties, the large mainframe computers were assembled in Poughkeepsie, with Endicott responsible for designing and manufacturing midrange computers. IBM introduced their personal computer in 1981—a huge departure from the way business had previously been conducted, as there were no sales personnel or field service people. The first operating system of IBM's personal computer was developed at IBM and known as DOS. IBM engaged young Bill Gates to develop an operating system for the personal computer (which he bought from another company for seventy-five thousand dollars), and to write the software for IBM's personal computers. Gates and his newly formed company Microsoft were free to market their software to anyone else. The microprocessor used in IBM's personal computers was purchased from Intel, who at that time was the leader in manufacturing microprocessors. Soon all the competing personal computer manufacturing companies were using the same microprocessor and the same software, so it became easy to connect a large number of personal computers together for the purpose of business communications, computing, and sharing information. IBM Endicott and the Glendale Development Lab became caught in the middle of these two competing market forces: the high-profit-margin, large-scale computers that were sold to big institutions and businesses along with bundled IBM developed software, and the low-profit-margin path of connecting a large number of personal computers together to do many of the same functions but at a much lower cost. The market for midrange computers dried up in the eighties and IBM Endicott's doors closed forever on July 1, 2002 (http://www.endicottalliance.org/news/endicottsale.htm). The IBM Endicott site was purchased by a group of local investors.

The purpose in revisiting my career years at IBM Endicott is to shed some understanding on how these machines (mainframe computers, handheld calculators, personal computers, minicomputers, and microcomputers) have slowly crept into our lives over the last half century to the point where they are now taking control of our daily lives.

When I started to work in 1968, IBM Endicott was the prime manufacturer of midsized computers, high-speed commercial business printers, and components that went into all of IBM's computers, such as the ceramic substrates that serve as the mounting base for the semiconductors as well as the printed circuit cards and boards that tie all the components together electrically. As an engineer, I spent the first six years of my career learning the processes that were used to manufacture the printed circuits. On the manufacturing floor, the printed circuits were made by contacting a silver emulsion-coated glass that contained the image of the circuit wires (working glass master) to a copper-foil-clad epoxy-glass panel that was coated with a photosensitive resist, exposing the resist to UV light, developing the resist, and then etching away the copper background, leaving only the thin copper wires, which served to electrically connect together all the components that would later be mounted on the board or card.

In the sixties and seventies, many of IBM's production machines were unique machines and were custom made by the equipment-engineering department. Of particular interest to me was the new photo tracing machine that was being developed at IBM Endicott when I arrived there in 1968. The development work on this machine was being done in the basement of Building 3. The machine was programmed to trace out each circuit line. Then it would stop, select a new reticle, and flash-expose each individual land (a square piece of real estate that served as the electrical connection between the circuit line and the drilled through hole) on the photosensitive coated piece of glass. After the tracing was complete, the glass was developed in standard photographic chemicals that develop silver emulsion films. The glass was coated with a protective coat, and then used in the manufacturing process to make multiple contact prints of a single layer of printed circuitry.

The light head on the photo tracing machine (PTM) remained stationary as the photosensitive glass (a glass plate coated with silver emulsion by Kodak) moved under the light head, thereby exposing the silver emulsion with a narrow beam of light. The unexposed glass master lay on a granite surface plate, and the position of the granite surface plate was moved around on a much larger piece of granite by a pair of programmable x-y motors. Of course, the commands to these x-y motors were given by an IBM Series 1 controller and a computer program that had been made by the artwork programming department. Of particular interest to me was the fact that the precise location of the unexposed silver emulsion plate was measured by a pair of laser interferometers. Thus, the accuracy of any x-y location on the glass master was determined in terms of wavelengths of light (very similar to the technology that I had worked on in graduate school). The table that held the glass master would begin to move, and then a computer program would open the aperture in the light head at the exact x-y location to begin or to end the scan of a printed circuit line. This circuit-generating technology allowed IBM to leap ahead of the competition and build some very large multilayer printed circuit boards that measured 15 by 17 inches. Later on, the artwork for even larger printed circuit boards was exposed on this machine by first tracing half of the pattern on the glass and then mechanically moving the glass so that the machine could trace out the other half of the glass. (The movement of IBM's original PTM 1 table was limited by the size of the interferometer mirrors commercially available at that time.) It was in this arena of generating glass masters, experimenting with different light projection systems, and contact printing the glass masters to the printed circuit boards that I felt most at home, because I was applying the physics that I had worked so hard and long to master in graduate school!

Before I go any further with my story of working at IBM, I would like to remind my readers that it takes many years for an invention (such as the laser, for example) to be reduced to some practical application that can be marketed, and then many more years to further reduce its cost so it can be marketed en masse. I recall my adviser in graduate school, Dr. Clifford Heer, being interviewed on the evening news in Columbus about the work that he was doing with masers and lasers at Ohio State University. At that time, there were many promises being made to apply the high frequency of the laser to high-speed communications. As I recall, he said that it would take perhaps twenty years before we would see lasers used in communications, and he was pretty much correct. Another example is the handheld calculator, which was invented by Jack Kirby at Texas Instruments around 1970, although its roots go way back to the invention of the transistor on December 16, 1947, at Bell Telephone Laboratories. The invention of the transistor is credited to William Shockley, John Bardeen, and Walter

Brattain, who were working at Bell Telephone Laboratories at the time. After Shockley left Bell Laboratories in 1950, he founded and served as director of the Shockley Transistor Corporation in Mountain View, California. The first transistors were made out of germanium. William Shockley began working on inventing a silicon transistor but abandoned his work. Several of his employees formed their own company, Fairchild Semiconductor Corporation, where the silicon-based transistor was invented. It was not until the 1960s that transistor radios began to appear on everyone's desk so that they could listen to their favorite radio stations or favorite music while they were working.

But the story doesn't end here. Two men, Robert Noyce and Jack Kirby, are credited with inventing the microchip around 1959; Noyce, who was one of the founders of Fairchild, and Kirby who was working for Texas Instruments at the time. After about ten years of legal wrangling, both were given credit for their earlier work by being awarded the National Medal of Science and inducted into the National Inventors Hall of Fame.

Kirby stayed at Texas Instruments and designed his own chips to make a handheld calculator called the Data-Math, which sold for $149.50 in 1970. Robert Noyce became unhappy with Fairchild in the midsixties, and he and Gordon Moore left, along with Andrew Grove, to found Intel in 1986. In 1969, an engineer at Intel named Ted Hoff managed to cram the logic into a single chip for a customer's desktop calculator (Busicom, a Japanese calculator manufacturer), thereby producing the world's first microprocessor. The design work and the rights to this microprocessor remained with Intel, who then sold it on the open market as the 4004, the forerunner of the entire 80x86 line of processors. Much of this early work can be read in "The History of Microprocessors" at www.jupiter.plymouth. edu/~harding/historymicro.html.

The events that I have just described in regard to the development of the transistor, integrated circuits, and microchips all gave rise to the invention of the first handheld calculator. I can remember reading in one of the electronics magazines while I was working at IBM in 1971 that Raman

Industries was going to introduce a handheld calculator that could add, subtract, multiply, divide, and calculate the square root of a number for less than a hundred dollars! Just imagine, a little handheld device that could perform all of the mathematics that I had struggled to memorize in my first eight grades of grammar school! I am not certain if Raman Industries ever released their handheld electronic calculator to the market or not, but it was at this time (circa 1971) that a number of companies like Texas Instruments and Hewlett Packard did release electronic calculators for the mass market. Along with the release of these first devices came the predictions that in five years, they would be selling in a blister pack in your grocery store for less than five dollars! Imagine, the entire math that you and I struggled to learn while in grammar school would now be available on a handheld device for less than five dollars! I didn't believe it then, but about fifteen years ago I purchased a rather large calculator from Walmart (on sale, of course) for a dollar. I used it for many years until the flex circuit that ran to the tilt-up readout gave out.

The educational and social aspects of the handheld calculator have become readily apparent today, when most young people cannot make change from a sale without a calculator or a sales terminal to do their thinking for them. But I am getting ahead of myself.

At this point in my career, around 1971, IBM was focused on building and selling large computers to universities for scientific work, and to large corporations and banks to record and store their financial transactions. If you wanted a handheld calculator, you purchased it for yourself. Nevertheless, the age of individuals having the power of a computer in their hands (even if it was just to add, subtract, multiply, or divide) was just beginning. In the seventies, IBM's solution to placing computer power in the hands of individuals was to sell to businesses an IBM mainframe computer along with desktop terminals and the necessary software so that a large number of individuals could use this one central computer at the same time. At Endicott, terminals (which consisted of a cathode ray tube and a full-sized keyboard) first started to show up on the desks of the production managers and their technicians, as well as the managers and technicians of all the departments associated with manufacturing. Then the terminals started showing up on the desks of the engineering department managers and finally on the desks of the engineers. These terminals were all interconnected with coaxial cables to a large central (IBM, of course) computer. IBM's various places of business were then connected together via large satellite dishes or phone lines that transmitted all the data from one location to another—or to anyplace in the world, for that matter. These terminals and computers were intended to be used for business purposes only: collecting and transmitting data to and from the production floor, tracking jobs on the manufacturing floor, or exchanging production information from one manufacturing site to another. Even though one could send a personal e-mail (communicate) for nonbusiness purposes over these systems, it was forbidden.

The terminals IBM produced were rather large and occupied about half of a normal 30-by-60-inch desktop. The readout was a cathode ray tube (just like those used in television sets of that period) and a full-size keyboard. And it was the keyboards that caused a big problem for manufacturing at IBM Endicott, because the Building 18 line produced multilayer circuit cards and boards only in 10-by-15-inch panel size. In the mid-seventies, Endicott set up a large panel line (known as the LPL) in Building 47 that was able to handle the 15-by-17-inch panel size. The printed circuits for two keyboards were manufactured on one LPL panel. The gold plating line also had to be resized for the LPL panels, as the key contacts required gold plating.

It was around 1975 that I accepted a job as a department manager. This was one of those "life-changing" decisions that came along, and I took the opportunity. It was a direction that I was not prepared to take. At that time IBM offered management positions to their top technical people, since they believed that management skills were something that could be taught in a school. It was a tough decision to make, because I had invested some ten years beyond my first twelve school years to become a physicist, but by becoming a manager, I had the opportunity to direct technical work and to influence the technical decision path. For the next fifteen years, I held a manager's position at IBM and greatly benefited from the many manage-ment schools that the company sponsored and all the special training ses-sions that managers were required to attend.

Toward the end of the seventies, the thinking at IBM Endicott was that there wasn't enough printed circuit-making capability in the entire world to produce what IBM needed for its expanding central computer/termi-nal business. This kind of thinking was brought on by the proliferation of central computers for everyday business purposes and the large number of terminals that were being connected to these centrally located computers. The other event that happened toward the end of the seventies was that the US government had finally closed its decade-long antitrust suit against IBM, and the company began to breathe some fresh air into its technical lungs after nearly a decade of slumber. IBM began building more plants worldwide in Austin, Texas; Research Triangle Park, North Carolina; and Sindelfingen, Germany, which essentially made the same kinds of products that were once exclusively made in Endicott, New York.

6

THE PERSONAL COMPUTER: IBM'S ORPHAN CHILD

BUT SOMETHING WAS about to happen that would change IBM and its play-ing field forever. In 1979, I was invited to attend IBM's VLSI (Very Large Scale Integration) Conference, which was held at the Westchester Country Club near New York City. This conference was arranged to summarize the work of those who were working on IBM's next generation of mainframe computers. Fishkill and Poughkeepsie were working on the semiconduc-tors and the multilayer ceramic modules. Each ceramic module supported 100 semiconductors and was cooled by liquid Freon. The multilayer board, which supported a total of nine modules, was being developed at Endicott. This new generation of multilayer boards, which I helped to develop, was 24 by 28 inches and contained twenty-two layers of circuitry (Bupp, J. R., L. N. Chellis, R. E. Ruane, J. P. Wiley, "High-Density Board Fabrication Techniques," *IBM Journal of Research and Development,* May 1982). The board program was code-named the Clark program, and Endicott's presentation was to be given by John Kresge, who was the functional development man-ager at the time.

It was at this conference that I learned about a group of engineers from Boca Raton, Florida, who had been given the responsibility of producing a personal computer which would sell for less than $1,400. There were a lot of snickers and chuckles in the conference hall when it was time for them to make their presentation. Manufacturing a personal computer which sold for less than $1,400? Was this some kind of a joke? And what did this have to do with VLSI computing? It was later that I learned about the huge debate going on in IBM's corporate management circles about the direction the company should take. On one side of the aisle were the traditional IBM people who made their living building and selling large mainframe computers to banks, businesses, and universities. These huge computers were accessed by many terminals that were owned by the institution that owned the central computer. These huge computers were powered by specialized semiconductors that used binary language. But the technology had changed, not because of IBM, but because huge numbers of semiconductors were being built for controller applications. These semiconductors used decimal language and were produced in large quantities, which made the price of a single semiconductor chip very, very cheap. Soon people realized that one could make a computer out of these controller chips for very little money. And if you could connect a whole bunch of small computers together, you could make a large computer! This group of engineers from Boca was very much despised by the people who were associated with the mainframe computers at IBM, because the marketing and sales path of the personal computer was that of a commodity, just as it was for the handheld calculator when it was introduced. And since the personal computer was headed toward becoming an electronic commodity sold to individuals just like the handheld calculator, there would be no need for a sales staff or a legion of repair specialists. The personal computer was to be sold at a store or in a catalog. No salesman to deal with. If it broke, you called an 800 number, and if that didn't solve your problem, you sent it back for another one. This was a game changer to IBM's culture. And it was a change that IBM could never financially accept, because the overhead structure of the mainframe computer was already in place.

It was Thomas J. Watson Jr., chairman of the board in 1967, who announced that IBM would open a large-scale manufacturing plant in Boca Raton to produce low- to moderately priced computers and business systems (www.bocahistory.org/our-history-ibm/). Watson's initial announcement gave Boca the manufacturing responsibility of producing System/360 Model 20 midsized computers. It wasn't until August 1981 that IBM launched a new product code named Acorn that put Boca Raton on the map. It was IBM's first personal computer, which was secretly developed by an engineering team led by William Lowe and then by Phillip "Don" Estridge (Boca Raton Historical Society & Museum, Boca Raton, Florida; http://www.bocahistory.org/our-history-ibm/).

At the time of the VLSI Conference in 1979, Thomas J. Watson Jr., IBM's chairman of the board and CEO, must have been acutely aware of the technology change that was being brought about by programming low-cost controller microprocessors to build a personal computer. It had to have been his decision to set aside some special funds and locate a group of engineers in the warm Florida sun at Boca Raton. This group of engineers was given the mission of coming up with a personal computer which sold for less than $1,400, and the project was to be funded separately, because any request for dollars through normal financial channels would have been instantly killed by those whose interests lay in the large mainframe computers, which brought in around fifty billion dollars of revenue a year for the company, a fact that no one could deny. The Boca group was also put at a distance from corporate management for another reason: they were given the responsibility for building a personal computer without the constraints of having to buy anything from any of the other IBM divisions. Thus, the CPU, motherboard, keyboards, memory cards, and power supplies could all be purchased from the lowest-cost supplier. This strategy was necessary for the Boca Raton group to meet their target cost objective. The rights of the operating system software were given (sold) to a young start-up named Bill Gates, who was working in a garage at the time. His company of course became Microsoft. The CPU (central processing unit) was Intel's 8088. Intel retained the manufacturing rights to sell the microprocessor to anyone else. Microsoft and Intel made tons of money on personal computers, but all that was left for IBM was to assemble its little machine and put it into a cardboard box that said "Intel Inside." IBM never made any money on the personal computer (as I remember, the PC Division was profitable for perhaps only two years in the early nineties), and eventually IBM's PC business was sold to Levono on December 8, 2004, for $1.25 billion in cash (www.commercetimes/story/38801.html).

I will never forget the VLSI Conference that I attended in 1979. John Kresge was a very likeable man but was terminally ill with leukemia. He partied the night before his speech like it was his last, thoroughly enjoying himself and recounting some of his whopper stories to anyone who would listen. The next morning I anxiously waited for John after I had my breakfast. He finally showed up at 8:45 a.m., just in time for his 9:00 a.m. presentation. I flipped through the foils for him as he gave his presentation. Within weeks of the VLSI Conference, John died at Roswell Park Hospital in Rochester, New York. Later, I received numerous phone calls from corporate headquarters demanding a copy of John's talk that he gave at the VLSI Conference, but there were no hard copies! Out of desperation, I borrowed a tape recorder, and one Sunday morning, I came to work and dictated John's presentation from the foils he had used. With the help of several of the secretaries, my dictation was turned into a hard copy. I admired John Kresge even though I never worked for him. He once told me to keep business and family separate, a good piece of advice that I later came to really appreciate. (Lesson Eleven: Business is business; family is family.) The longer I stayed with IBM, the clearer his wisdom became. In the 1980s, it started to become obvious that the company's decisions were being made for the good of the corporation and not for the good of the employees, even though IBM championed such phrases as *respect for the individual, think, and full employment policy.*

7

ADAPTATION OF THE PERSONAL COMPUTER AT IBM

EVEN THOUGH IBM introduced its own line of personal computers in 1981, their usage at the Endicott site came about very slowly. All of its internal business needs were satisfied by having terminals connected to a central computer, which in turn was connected to computers at other IBM locations. The terminals were used for normal office communication within the company but not outside of the company. The software we used was produced by IBM and had been generated for sale to other companies. It was called PROFS (Professional Office Systems). This software allowed anyone to generate, send, file, and print e-mail correspondence to anyone in the company. A copy of the correspondence could be sent to a central printer if one needed a hard copy, as the days of the personal printer had not yet arrived.

In the mideighties, my office computer was replaced with an IBM personal computer, but for the most part, the personal computers were used as "dumb terminals." We had not only a monitor (cathode ray–type monitor) and a keyboard on our desks, but also a lot of wires running to the computer box, which resided under our desks. But slowly the usage of the personal computer began to pick up as it became a necessary tool for both manage-ment, who used company-generated programs to do their correspondence and employee evaluations, and the engineers, who began to use programs generated by outside companies that allowed them to do spreadsheet calcu-lations and more sophisticated engineering design tasks such as CAD (com-puter assisted design). It was at this juncture that department secretaries disappeared and those who remained were assigned to third-level managers or above and known as "administrative assistants." Manufacturing data such as quantities manufactured, yields, unit hour targets, and costs were all col-lected and displayed on personal computers for managers and engineers alike. IBM partnered with AT&T to transmit data across AT&T's phone lines, and from that point on, work data for IBM employees was available at employees' homes. IBM made it even easier to work at home with the introduction of its laptop computers. But just like the first handheld calcu-lators, they were assigned to individual engineers and managers and had to be locked up at night in their docking stations. (A rather large steel bicycle cable with a padlock did the trick!) Managers could take their computers home at night and read their e-mail or review the latest production data. And the engineers started to use the laptops in all sorts of imaginative ways.

In 1985 I became functional manager of the Endicott photo lab, which was responsible for generating and processing all the glass masters for the Endicott site. At that time, the photo lab had a backlog of four thousand orders for production glass! And they operated on a priority system that was meant to confuse the customer. An order for a glass master would bounce back and forth between the department that received the order and the department that generated the numerical date and then finally go to the production control department, which set the priority for the order and was responsible for releasing it to the photo lab for build. Naturally, a bro-ken glass that was holding up an order on the manufacturing floor received top priority, and orders for development glass masters were at the bottom of the priority scheme. All the communication was done by sending let-ters in triplicate through the company's internal mail system, and it took several days just to move a letter from one department to another. The time had come for an e-mail ordering system, which I facilitated by writing a white paper about the delays caused by the old "memo in triplicate" order-ing system.

At the same time, production orders for the Clark boards were on the rise, and the photo tracing machine (PTM 1) was hopelessly out of date. When the Clark program first started, it might take the PTM 1 a whole day to generate just one single layer on a piece of glass. But as the program became more mature and the line density increased, run times stretched out to two and three days. Summer thunderstorms often came through Endicott around 4:00 p.m., and one brief interruption of the electrical power to the photo tracing machine when it was generating a piece of art-work would cause the glass to be scrapped and the program to be restarted all over from the beginning on a new piece of glass.

Stark Roberts was given the responsibility of overseeing the building of a new photo lab and a new family of photo tracing machines for the Clark program. Stark was a navy pilot during WWII, and like most of the men who came through that era, he was a no-bullshit kind of person. Although he had worked more than forty years at IBM Endicott, he had maintained a remark-able sense of humor. Stark's favorite saying became one of my favorites, too. (Lesson Twelve: There are old pilots and there are bold pilots, but there are no old, bold pilots.) He was one of the few managers I have ever known who was given the necessary resources to accomplish the objectives that he had been assigned. Don Moses headed the equipment build function at River Plaza, Pat Walsh headed the programming function, Tom Atherton headed the mainte-nance function, and I headed the photo lab function. As best as I can remem-ber, Stark had some nine hundred people reporting to him. Stark also set the objective to have the new photo lab operate entirely without paper: no paper routings, no paper process specifications, yields and unit hour tracking online, operator training manuals online, and so on. It was a massive undertaking. And that is why he needed the programming function to achieve that objective. The next four years were to be my most enjoyable and productive years at IBM.

As I said previously, the original PTM 1 was hopelessly out of date. The follow-on machine, PTM II, was built at River Plaza but was subsequently shipped to Singlefingen, Germany. PTM III was built in the River Plaza build shop but couldn't be moved to Endicott, because it was immediately pressed into service at the River Plaza build site to keep the supply of Clark glass masters flowing to the production line. A second PTM III was completed at River Plaza. By this time the space in the new Building 53 photo lab was ready for the first PTM III to be installed in its clean room. Later, the second PTM III was also moved into Building 53 at the Endicott complex.

The machines that traced out the lines and lands for the Clarke boards were very complex and were required to run flawlessly for several days to generate a single layer of circuitry. Even though there were many checks built into these machines, it was still necessary to frequently check on their progress and to see if they were still operating. One of the engineers, Les Mayes, used his laptop computer to keep a check on the photo tracing machines (PTM) while at home. He could connect via a phone line to the computer that was running the PTM (I believe it was a Series 1) and determine if the machines were operational or needed some kind of intervention. If he could, he would try to restart the machine from home, and if that didn't work, he would come into work and troubleshoot the problem. Keep in mind that these machines worked twenty-four hours a day, seven days a week, and monitoring them from home was a very efficient way of keeping track of their progress. Soon, one began to see more and more engineers taking their work home at night or working on special assignments using their laptop computers during off-hours. In most cases, IBM would reimburse you for the expense of your home phone line if your manager thought that you needed it for business. (This was about fifteen years before phone companies learned how to run both phone conversations and computer data over the same copper wire, so if you were using your phone to connect up your computer, you couldn't talk on your telephone unless you had a second line.) It was in the early nineties that most people became connected to the Internet and to each other via their personal computers. If you had a personal computer and a telephone line, you now had access to all kinds of real-time information and stored data, and you could literally communicate with anyone in the entire world!

8

MACHINES THAT DO OUR
WORK AND OUR THINKING

I WANT TO leave my days at IBM and examine what this new technology has done to us from both a learning standpoint and a social standpoint. How do we learn? As children, we learn by experience and repetition. When we touch a hot object such as a stove, we instantly feel the pain the heat causes. And because we have minds that remember, we associate stoves with heat and pain, and never indiscriminately touch a hot stove again. If we bump into an object such as a big rock, we receive a bruise and remember not to bump into that object again. Much of my grammar school learning was accomplished by memorization (repetition). In my grammar school days, we spent evenings memorizing lists of words so we could spell them correctly the next day on the spelling test. That was how spelling was taught in those days although my mother, who was a schoolteacher, said that the proper way to learn to spell a word was to pronounce it first (she would say, "sound it out") and then try to spell it. Much of the mathematics teaching in grades four, five, and six was accomplished by memorization. Do any of you remember the flash cards that teachers used to teach math? Keep repeating something often enough and it finally sticks in your mind. Today's politicians use repetition to teach us who to vote for by planting enough signs along the road or running the same commercial over and over again so that when it comes time to vote, we vote for their names even though we don't remember anything about them!

Repetition works particularly well when learning a sport. When I was in grammar school, we learned to play basketball in the gymnasium. At first one's skills are very minimal, but if you shoot that basketball enough times, eventually it will go through the hoop. And if you keep practicing, the percentage of shots that go through the hoop slowly begins to increase. Repetition as a learning skill does not stop in grammar school. We are in awe of the professional golfers who, when playing a tournament, make one perfect swing after another, but most of these golfers know that they have to practice each day, and some of the really top names, like Tiger Woods, make it a habit to swing a golf club at least a thousand times a day! They make the game seem easy when you see them play, but to them it's a lot of hard work.

Training our minds to recognize danger, learn skills, solve problems, or just remember all the information taught to us in school is the basis of our learning. I found that I could remember things best if I associated an image with what I wanted to remember. For example, when driving a car, my mind stores images of places along the way. This type of memory tool does have its shortcomings because I have a terrible time remembering the name of someone I have just met, although I will never forget the person's face.

It is because we can see, sense, and remember that we learn. Certainly the engineers who work on our military arsenal understand how humans learn and have applied those principles to many of our modern weapons. For example, cruise missiles are programmed with the images of the terrain that they are to follow, and as a cruise missile flies along the predetermined route, an onboard computer compares the real-time camera images with the programmed images. The missile's flight is then adjusted accordingly. This technique allows the missile to fly very close to the ground or to weave in and out of valleys and mountainous terrain as it flies along its programmed route. It's really sort of the same technique that I use when I am driving to a place that I have previously visited.

Our Predator drones are designed as a combination of a pilotless airplane and a pilot who sits at some remote location. These planes do not have a human aboard, but they can take off, fly to their target, fire a missile, and then return to their home base. They are flown by a pilot who sits behind a computer screen and sees exactly what the television camera on the drone plane is seeing. No more worrying about G-suits, oxygen masks, or being shot down by enemy fire. All of the fighting is done from the comforts of the command room.

IBM recently celebrated the fifteenth anniversary of their Deep Blue computer beating world champion Garry Kasparov master chess player on May 11, 1997 (www.engadget.com/2012/05/11/ibm-deep-blue-anniversary/). Chess is an intellectual game of strategy, based on anticipating your opponent's next move. But now what's the point of playing the game when a machine can beat the best of the best chess players? I remember when I was in seventh grade, our teacher, Mr. Hicks, often played checkers with his students during noon recess. On a few occasions, one of us would win, but we all knew that he didn't really have to lose. He did indeed let us win occasionally just so he would have someone to play checkers with!

Many of the sensors that are used in some commercial machines today came from the development of military weaponry. Several years ago Jeanette, my second wife, received an iRobot Roomba vacuum cleaner from her daughter for Christmas. This little machine vacuums your floor while you sit on the couch and watch television. It was developed by the iRobot Corporation, which developed the technology for robots that can go into a building and search for a bomb or an armed fugitive. This little vacuum cleaner is round in shape and has been programmed to make spiral moves when it bumps into something. It's fun to watch the machine when it is working under the kitchen table and becomes trapped by all the table and chair legs. It bumps into the legs, spins a little, moves in another direction until it finds an opening, and then scoots across the floor to vacuum another section of the room. It finds its way out of these predicaments by trial and error, much like your children find their way out of a corn maze at Halloween time. The little machine is a great work saver, and because it is only four inches high, it can scoot under beds and under the sofa—places where an ordinary vacuum cleaner cannot reach unless you move the furniture, and of course, that's a lot of work!

It wasn't until November 2010 that I came to the stark realization of how much of our everyday thinking is now being done by machines. I was in the market for a new car, because a deer had run into the side of my old Toyota Camry and essentially totaled it. I went to the Toyota dealership fully intending to buy another Camry. I sat in a new Camry, and it felt much like the one I had been driving. And then the salesman asked, "Why don't you sit in one of our new Prius models?" From the moment I sat in the Prius, I knew that this car was something different. It was a second-generation Prius Hybrid, which is designed to get the best gas mileage of any car on the road. Just sitting in a Prius makes you feel like you are sitting in an airplane cockpit! The instrument panel and controls had to be designed by "kids" who learned their trade from playing video games after school. I had not been so excited about a car since I was a teenager, and I rushed home to get my wife, Jeanette, to take a look at it. Everything about the Prius is different. It has been designed for maximum fuel efficiency and consistently delivers fifty miles per gallon, regardless of where you drive it. I bought the car without test-driving it, and in a few days, we returned to the dealership to pick it up. It was in the dark of evening when we arrived at the dealership. The salesman showed us some of the car's features while it was parked in the garage. With the salesman aboard, we took a little test-drive around the block before we left for home. At home, I parked the car in the garage, but I couldn't remember how to turn it off, because there is no ignition switch! I took the stack of manuals into the house and began to read the operating instructions. I was able to locate the power button and shut off the car for the night.

The controls in this car take some getting used to, because they do not always follow the usual automotive conventions. Starting the vehicle always requires you to put your foot on the brake first and then push the power button. There is no key, just a little black electronic box you keep in your pocket. You unlock the driver's door by pulling on the door handle as though the car wasn't locked at all. To lock the car, you just squeeze the driver's door handle and the doors lock. For two weeks after we bought the car, I would still find myself reaching for the key in the ignition switch to start it or shut it off. And "park" is not a part of the shift mechanism; it's a little button on the console! I am still having trouble with that park button. Fortunately, the car is smart enough to put itself into park automatically when you turn off the power button. But if you forget to put the car into park (push the *P* button), and get out of the car to get the mail, it will roll forward in drive!

Do you remember when you were a teenager and came to a stoplight and wanted to impress your friends with the power of your car? You put the gearshift in neutral, revved up the engine (*vroom, vroom, vroom*), suddenly dropped the transmission shifter into drive, and away you went, screeching tires and all. Well, you can try that one with a Prius, but you won't get any response! If you step on the gas while the transmission is in neutral, it simply ignores you, because it has been programmed for maximum gas mileage, and stepping on the accelerator when in neutral is a sure gas waster. At this point I realized that there was no mechanical connection between the accelerator and the engine. All of your commands are received by electronic sensors and then converted into action by electric motors. And if you try to do something dumb, the car just ignores you!

Just after I had taken delivery of my Prius, the Toyota Motor Corporation received some bad news that one of its Lexus hybrid models unexpectedly sped up and eventually crashed at high speed, killing everyone aboard. But remember, there are no mechanical connections between the steering wheel and the front tires, between the brake pedal and the brakes, or between the accelerator pedal and the engine. At first this realization was a very scary thought for me, and we wondered if we shouldn't take this car back to the dealer and trade it for something a little more conventional. I did a little experimenting on my own. On the Prius, the gearshift lever has been replaced by a "joystick." You put the car into drive by once again step-ping on the brake, and then moving the joystick to the *D* position. Releasing the joystick, it returns to the center neutral position. If you try to move the joystick to the neutral position when you are driving, the car ignores you. (If you hold the joystick in neutral for a few seconds, the transmission eventually will go into neutral.) You can press the power button when you are driving at speed, and again, the car ignores your commands. So you can imagine the panic that the driver of that Lexus must have felt as he tried to gain control of his car. The only thing left for him was to jam on the brakes, which he did until they burned out. But the car kept accelerating and finally crashed at 125 mph. (Much later, the Toyota Corporation revealed that if you put one foot on the accelerator and one foot on the brake, the com-puter will completely disengage the engine from the driver's controls. But that is certainly not conventional motorcar-driving wisdom.) Maybe it's a male thing, but I like to have some control over the mechanical things that I operate. But then I began thinking about the pilots of our passenger planes and our military planes. There are no cables or wires connecting the pilot's hands and arms to the control surfaces of the airplane. The control surfaces are actuated by electric motors, which respond only to the elec-tronic signals that originate from the pilot. Our newest military jet fighter is so unstable that only a computer is fast enough to sense the corrections needed to keep the aircraft under control and on a steady course. But this is just another sign that the human pilot is rapidly becoming obsolete.

I bought the lowest-cost Prius, but for more money, I could have pur-chased one with additional electronics such as "Intelligent Parking Assist," which will automatically parallel park your car, or "Lane Keep Assist," which will keep your Prius in its own lane when you are driving, or "Dynamic Radar Cruise Control/Pre-Collision System," which automatically adjusts the speed of your car to keep a preset distance between it and the car in front of you. Of course my Prius has antilock brakes. I really wouldn't buy a car without this safety feature, especially because we live in snow country. (You do remember being taught in driver's education how to prevent a skid by pumping your brakes, don't you?) Soon, all of these safety features will become standard on all cars.

Not only have machines taken over the work that once belonged to men before the Industrial Revolution, but they are taking away the thinking that we once had to do to operate these machines and to survive in society. The human body tires out and loses strength, our nervous system cannot react fast enough to a deer crossing the road, and our minds don't have enough storage capacity to remember all the things that we have been taught over the course of our lifetimes. But now the combination of machine and computer exceeds the limits of human frailty and mental capacity.

The human mind is structured much like the serial processor of a computer: it can concentrate on only one thought at a time, even though the folks who teach time management want you to "multitask" by trying to do several things at once. If you are driving a vehicle, you had better be concentrating on your driving! According to a 2008 study by the National Highway Traffic Safety Administration and the Virginia Tech Transportation Institute, 80 percent of crashes and 65 percent of near-crashes involve some form of driver distraction. I cringe when I drive down the road from my house to Canandaigua, because I pass many, many cars in which the drivers are looking down and not even looking at the road! (We live very near Finger Lakes Community College in Canandaigua, and most of these drivers are young students texting while driving.) I fear for my life. I want to blow my horn or shout, "Wake up, you idiot, I am on this road too!" Texting and using a cell phone while driving is not permitted in New York State, because both of your hands must be free to hold on to the steering wheel, but the law is violated all the time. Many of the male contractors I observe use their cell phones while driving their pickup trucks to set up a new job or to find out if the materials they ordered have been received. But for the most part, these men are at least looking at the road when they drive. The women drivers are just as guilty of using cell phones while driving. I see them driving with a phone pressed to their left ear so they won't miss a single word of the conversation. We all know and can cite many examples of the disastrous results of trying to do two things at once, especially when driving a car. Our everyday technology has not fully caught up to the limitations of the human body and mind, and although we keep passing laws to try to fill the gaps, most drivers just ignore them.

9

A Tsunami Wave of Social Disruption Has Landed!

In 1974, ARCHAEOLOGISTS found what they believed to be the oldest remains of our human ancestors. The remains are those of a female they have named Lucy. Lucy lived some 3.2 million years ago near Hadar, Ethiopia, and stood perhaps three and a half feet tall. While I was visiting my daughter Michele and her family in Gastonia, North Carolina, we visited a museum nearby that had a display of what scientists thought Lucy might have looked like. My first impression was that Lucy was not very much like us today and that if I had held out my hand to her, she would have bitten off my fingers before I could have blinked. According to Alvin Toffler (1980) in his book *The Third Wave*, the agricultural wave of society emerged some ten thousand years ago. Before that, people lived in small groups and fed themselves by foraging, fishing, hunting, or herding animals. Man has had at least ten thousand years to develop the skills necessary to live in small villages, take care of the land, and cultivate what was necessary to sustain his own life, the lives of his family, and those of his animals.

Contrast the agricultural society to the industrial society, which began around 1650, some 360 years ago. Man began to transition himself away from the land and from small villages to larger villages and factories that were first run by water power and then by steam power. These larger villages were interconnected by the steam locomotive, which was used to transport the raw materials and the finished products. But even in the period right up to 1900, some 41 percent of the workforce in the United States were still engaged in some kind of agricultural activity.

In the first part of this book I trace some of the key inventions that have brought computing to the masses of people. These key inventions, which started to be recorded a little after the end of the Second World War, are enabling a whole series of new machines whose performance is vastly different from what we have previously known. I believe that we have entered a new phase of the Industrial Revolution. In the first part of the Industrial Revolution, man's muscles were replaced by machines that dug into the earth, transported raw materials and finished goods, and moved anything that was too heavy for him to lift. But in this second phase of the Industrial Revolution, we are creating machines that not only do our work but are beginning to do our thinking for us! In my opinion, we are not into the Third Wave of Civilization that Alvin Toffler writes about in *The Third Wave*. No, what we are experiencing is merely a logical extension of the industrial society. But the effect is huge, and it feels like we have been hit by a giant tidal wave of disruption that has turned our families, our thinking, our educational systems, our politicians, our lives, and even our religious views upside down.

In my view this tsunami wave of disruption really started to come ashore in 1981, around the time IBM introduced its first personal computer. Yes, I know there were other makers of personal computers before IBM came onto the market—makers such as Atari and Commodore who made machines for children to play games on. Each time these manufacturers brought out a new machine, you needed to buy new software to run it, and the software from one manufacturer was not interchangeable with the software from another. But the games were fun, and kids loved to play pretend tennis or Pac-Man on their computers.

It was IBM who gave the personal computer its legitimacy in the business world and eventually in the consumer world by standardizing the microprocessor and the software that ran it, much like what happened in the very early days of the railroad when someone decided to standardize the distance between the steam engine's wheels and the distance between the rails. We did not feel this tsunami wave of technology all at once. In fact it was spread out over a period of perhaps ten years, from the time the IBM personal computer was introduced (1981) to the time personal computers were found in most homes and were being connected to each other via telephone lines (around 1991). As the Internet build-out started to gain speed during the early 1990s, more and more of the world's data stored in libraries, universities, museums, and government archives became digitalized. By the end of the 1990s, our children were rapidly gaining access to all kinds of information just by clicking the computer's mouse. If we look back on this electronics revolution, we realize that children have taken the lead in using this new technology to share information. They have adapted it as their own, fought with their parents over it, and then carried it to new heights of personal communication that have never been experienced before in the history of man. All of this has occurred while they were having fun with the new technology, playing games and sending e-mail and text messages to their friends. But sadly, along with this new mode of communication came the decline of personal interaction. When was the last time you saw children playing outside together, other than at games organized by adults?

The real social casualties of this tsunami of technical revolution are those of us who have lost our jobs and our leadership roles as heads of society's institutions. Let me give you an example of how machines have taken over our jobs. When I was the functional manager of the photo lab at IBM Endicott around 1985, we were hard at work trying to bring all aspects of processing silver emulsion glass plates up to date. Before this time, all silver emulsion glass masters were developed in a tray by an operator using cloth wipes to agitate the solution and a clock to keep track of the time spent in a particular tray. But with the Clark technology, it now took days for a machine to trace out one single circuit layer on a single piece of

22.5-by-26.5-inch glass plate. We desperately needed an automatic plate processor controlled by a microprocessor that would give consistent developing results as long as the chemistry in the baths was properly maintained. With a plate processor, all an operator had to do was load the glass into the machine and press the start button.

But you would not believe the pushback I received from the photo lab operators. After many meetings of trying to convince them why we needed to make this change, I finally received some feedback from my second-level manager: the operators opposed this change because it would take away their "artistic ability" to make changes to the developing process when they felt such changes were needed. What they were really saying to me was "You are taking away my job, which I have spent many, many years learning." Several years later, after we installed the plate processor, the operators finally concluded that the plate processor did a much better technical job of developing the photographic plates than they could do manually, and they actually thanked me for backing the installation of this piece of equipment. But they were right: it did eventually cost them their jobs, because it took only a few people to run the entire photo lab. Most were moved to other jobs in the photo lab or to other jobs in manufacturing.

But this was just the tip of the iceberg, as all of IBM's manufacturing lines and their associated processes were being updated with machines that were controlled by microprocessors. This revolution happened in the electronics industry as well as in the car-assembly industry and in all kinds of manufacturing environments. Machines that were controlled by microprocessors were fast replacing the old jobs that had been done by human operators. The machines never tired and never complained; they just kept doing what they had been programmed to do. Our politicians keep talking about the loss of jobs and the devastation that has occurred to the middle class, but they never seem to blame the real culprit: the automation of manufacturing and of many service jobs such as elevator operators, telephone operators, service station attendants, and bank tellers; the list keeps growing longer and longer.

This revolution in automation did not stop with the manufacturing worker. No indeed! It rolled right into the engineering jobs that supported manufacturing. It was a long time coming, but the jobs that were previously done by the industrial engineering department—process routings, yields, calculating unit hours, and adding them up for a particular job—could now be placed in a computer and the data collected automatically as the product was manufactured. The specifications that used to be manually written were now entered into the computer by the engineer and placed online for preapproval and then for all of the manufacturing operators to read. Production control, which schedules the introduction of parts into manufacturing, could now do their job online. Everyone was now able to see the location of all the orders in the manufacturing line and to follow a critical order as it progressed through the line. Management could review yields each day and redirect resources if a problem occurred. The revolution spread to the designers, who now designed the actual part on a CAD (computer assisted design) terminal/computer, which contained programmed rules of design. Once finished and approved, the design of the new part could be transported anywhere in the world. Gone were the legions of draftsmen and rooms of filing cabinets that contained the latest EC (engineering change) paper design. If a design change was required, all the designer had to do was make the change in the CAD system with a few clicks of the mouse, and then release it to the manufacturing system so that the new change was instantly available all around the world.

It didn't take long for this technical revolution to almost completely destroy the family unit. During my years of growing up on the family farm, all the members of our family ate three meals together every day, seven days a week. Mealtime was a time to refuel your body, rest up from the work of the day, and discuss with parents what had happened at school. And then after dinner, we would all watch the news on the TV and then perhaps be entertained by one of the evening TV shows like Groucho Marx's *You Bet Your Life* or *I Love Lucy*.

During my working years, I felt very fortunate and proud that I was able to earn enough money working at IBM to buy a home, raise my family, and eat most of my evening meals with the family. I made enough money so that my wife Dianna could stay at home with our children Michael and Michele as they grew up, and she did not have to work outside the home to help support the family. How different family life is today, when most families have two working parents. Much of our economy today is based upon service jobs, which pay perhaps ten dollars per hour or about twenty thousand dollars per year. Even if both husband and wife work, they can barely meet a very minimal standard of living. And even if the family does have one or two working professionals, their jobs demand long commutes or absence from the home for extended periods of time. Most of today's working families depend upon day care facilities to bring up their children while they are working. Some families are lucky enough to have their grandparents living nearby whom often help to bring up the children.

For many working married couples, sharing a meal together today is almost impossible, because one parent has to pick up the children from day care or from the grandparent's home while the other is out shopping for something to eat. And when the children do become old enough to go to school, one parent has to take the children to extracurricular activities like dance lessons, or karate, or soccer so that the children can have some scheduled exercise and to keep them occupied when they are not in the classroom. How many times did I hear this cell phone conversation at Wegmans (the grocery store where I worked part-time): "Honey, what do you want for dinner tonight?" No time to plan, no time to talk or to sit down at the table together for a meal; only enough time to pick up the children from day care, grab something off the grocery store shelf for dinner, and then rush home to heat it on the stove, feed the children, put them to bed, and collapse from exhaustion so that they can do the same thing again the next day.

And this same disruption has rolled along into our churches. With many parents working in retail, attending church on Saturday night or on Sunday as a family is all but impossible. And now, many schools are scheduling athletic events on Sundays! So with this flurry of working at retail jobs, working out of town, or transporting the children to and from athletic events on weekends, is it any wonder that our church pews are empty of families with children?

10

WILL MAN BECOME OBSOLETE?

I HAVE TO ask the question: Is man becoming obsolete in this fast-paced technical world that he has created for himself? Or, as my mother would say to me, "Has he become too smart for his own good?" I think I have made some very good technical arguments about how the human body and mind can no longer handle many of the situations that we routinely have to deal with in the world we live in today. Probably one of the better-known examples is space exploration work. That work is being done by robots, which can survive in environments where man would instantly perish.

I never entertained the thought that I would someday become obsolete when I was growing up on the family farm. My experience was just the opposite: I was an integral part of a family unit that raised its own food and then sold what we didn't need for ourselves or the animals to earn money for the family unit. By the time the fifties rolled around, the Industrial Revolution was rapidly changing the agricultural scene. Tractors were in wide use, as well as harvesting machines such as combines, hay bailers, corn pickers, silage harvesters, and so on—all pulled by a single tractor. And there were gravity box wagons and elevators, which did much of the backbreaking work of moving the bales of hay, ears of corn, or harvested grain into the barn for storage during the winter months. We milked our cows with a Surge milking machine so that two men each with a machine could milk about thirty dairy cows in about an hour.

But even with all this equipment, we were never without work to do on the farm. There were always the cows to be milked twice a day, the chickens to be fed and the eggs to be gathered, and the hogs to be slopped. And then after breakfast, the barns needed to be cleaned, or the fields needed to be planted, or the crops needed to be harvested. There was plenty of work to do all year around. In the winter the straw sheds that housed the dairy cows needed to be cleaned, and the harvesting equipment needed to be serviced or repaired. This first phase of industrial farm equipment allowed a family to care for perhaps one hundred to two hundred acres of land, but the entire family was integral to the working unit. And it didn't matter if the day on the calendar was Sunday or a holiday: the cows still needed to be milked, the chickens fed and the eggs gathered, and the hogs slopped. Yet, as a family, we had time to eat three meals together every day, to go to church on Sunday morning, and to work the fields only during the week. We boys had time to play softball in the pasture on Sunday afternoon or to go swimming in the neighbor's pond in the summer or ice skating in the winter, or to shoot a few basketballs into the hoop that hung in Grandmother's barn. My parents never planned our recreational activities for us, nor did they take time off from their work to take us to recreational activities after school.

During the seventies and the early eighties, IBM did a very good job of keeping its workforce employed. The company would offer individuals retraining for another job at the same location or perhaps a transfer to another location that needed more workers. Sometimes the retraining would be extensive and you would be sent to school to learn entirely new skills or to even to college to earn a degree that would help you advance your career within the company. Full-time employment was not guaranteed at IBM, but for a long time in my career, the company did a good job of balancing its work requirements within the company and retraining its employees when the technology changed or when sales slowed. And in return, the company enjoyed a great loyalty among its workers.

It wasn't until 1994 that IBM Endicott had its first layoff (www.endicottalliance.org/news/jobactions.htm). During the mideighties, IBM would offer its older employees early retirement when sales began to slow. They would offer you a lump sum of money (say, two years' worth of salary) spread over a period of four years if you would take early retirement. It was no coincidence that the adaptation of the personal computer in the workplace corresponded with IBM's early retirement policies and the layoffs that followed. The simple fact was that it didn't take as many people to do the work, including the manufacturing. Manufacturing became more and more automated, as did the work done by all kinds of professional people such as secretaries, engineers, and designers. They were easily replaced by computer programs or machines that contained microprocessors.

It was in the nineties that I personally started to feel that I was becoming obsolete at IBM. I took early retirement in April 1998, but I really didn't want to retire, because I felt that I still had a lot to contribute technically to IBM—or to any other technology company, for that matter. I had spent twenty-two years of my life in school earning my degrees just so I could work for a company like IBM. But toward the end of my career, all large companies were handling their engineering hires with specific projects in mind. The job descriptions were very carefully worded and narrowly focused in regard to skills. If you didn't have those skills, you were not a candidate for the job. And if you did get a job, once the project was over, you and your job were gone. There would be no money for retraining or moving to another location within the company.

11

WHAT DO PEOPLE
REALLY WANT?

WHEN MY FIRST book came out (*The Last of the Family Farms*), I arranged a number of book signings to promote it. One of those book signings was at the Gorham Free Library in Gorham, New York. I live in Gorham, a predominantly rural township that still has many active farms. Several people who attended my presentation were still actively engaged in agriculture. Many others had grown up on a farm or at least still lived in the country. After I finished my presentation, the hostess, Diane Hovey, asked the audience, "If you could use only one word to describe what it was like to grow up on a farm, what would it be?" Some of the answers were *nature, the land*, and *the animals*. But then she went on to say that for her, it was the freedom that she experienced when she was growing up on their family farm. Now, that comment took me by complete surprise. I briefly recalled my days on the farm and how my mother and father never took any vacation: there were cows to be milked, chickens to be fed, and hogs to be slopped twice a day, 365 days of the year. And then there were crops and the garden to be planted in the spring, hay to be made in the summer, and corn to be picked in the fall. *Freedom?* Our family was tied to the farm, and to the animals and the land, which depended upon us to do our job each day. But the more I think about her comment, the more I think she got it right. As farmers, our raw materials were the land, the rain, the sun, and the animals. Our real clock was the sun, and our only real boss was the Almighty Himself. Were there risks? Sure. Sometimes the Lord did not send enough sun or rain and the crops withered, or the animals became sick, or we got sick, or the market for milk would be down, which affected the family's income. But at least we had some control over our lives. If you worked harder, you could produce more. Your table was always spread with fresh milk, eggs, meat, and vegetables that were grown right on the farm. There was enough time to go to school during the week, go shopping on Saturday, go to church on Sunday, and to visit relatives or just rest on Sunday afternoon before the start of a new week.

The idea of freedom was embedded in the founding of this country by Thomas Jefferson when on July 4, 1776; he delivered the Declaration of Independence to the newly formed Congress and used the words *life, liberty, and the pursuit of happiness*. Yes, these are the goals and objectives that we Americans have been pursuing since the beginning of our county. But I as well as many others sense that we are fast losing ground in our pursuit of these goals.

As a result of the Industrial Revolution, machines have taken over most of our manual labor. All kinds of machines: diesel ships and trains to move the raw materials and finished goods, bulldozers, track hoes, and earth movers to build our ditches and roadways, steam turbines to run our generators to power our factories that make the products that we use every day. The gasoline engine replaced our horses with tractors and our carriages with cars. And because the gasoline engine could produce a great deal of power in a relatively small, lightweight package, man learned to fly and was no longer tied to the Earth! All of these changes came about in the United States from the early 1800s until the early 1900s—a very short period of only a hundred years! But being human, our bodies still need exercise, so man has had to seek out other forms of exercise to keep him healthy. Today our exercise and eating habits, which have evolved from our lifestyles, are not good enough to maintain healthy bodies. You see it in our young. Walk to school? I guess not. It's either ride the bus or be driven to school by parents or friends. When was the last time you saw any of your neighbor's children playing outside after school? I actually saw some Old Order Mennonite children playing outside their one-room schoolhouse this winter in Gorham, and I wanted to stop and take a picture. It brought back a flood of memories of when I went to school in the forties and fifties and we too played outside during the morning and afternoon recesses and during lunchtime. Today, parents have to take their children to some organized exercise programs such as dancing, karate, or a multitude of sports programs that are run by the schools during week nights and on the weekends. We have left it up to our schools to provide not only learning, but exercise, nutrition, and a safe environment for our children, because most parents are much too busy just trying to make a living.

In this new age that began just before the start of the twenty-first century, machines are beginning to take over our thinking for us. What is this going to do to the development of the human mind and a man's ability to think and to create new things? When I was growing up in the forties and fifties, our parents, our Sunday school teachers, and our schoolteachers did much of our decision making (thinking) for us. Making our own decisions didn't come until we were ready to leave home or go to college. But now the television teaches the children their basic colors, the alphabet, how to play, what toys to play with, and how to interact with other children. It also tells them what to believe, and what to ask Mom and Dad for at Christmas! Unfortunately, the producers of these TV programs all have a hidden agenda. And their agenda is paid for by the advertiser.

The widespread use of the calculator in the seventies eliminated the need for our children to learn mathematics in elementary school. No more memorizing math tables with flash cards like I did in the fourth and fifth grade. And with the introduction of the personal computer around 1981 and the general build-out of the Internet in the early 1990s, our children don't really have to work very hard at remembering anything, because most of man's knowledge since the beginning of time has been digitized and stored somewhere on a computer disk which can be easily looked up on the internet.

By combining machines and computers, we have entered into a new age where the machines can react much faster than you or I can, they can remember far more than you and I will ever remember in our lifetimes, and their speed of making decisions is increasing according to Moore's Law (circa 1960), which says that computing power will double every year. Unfortunately, humans haven't improved much in their strength or intelligence in the last several hundred thousand years!

The Industrial Revolution has freed us from much backbreaking physical work, but now the machines that we invented are slowly taking away our decision-making capability. I am very concerned that we could easily become slaves to these machines we have created! Let me give you a couple of examples of the absolute control that these machines are exerting over us, examples that no doubt you have observed in your family. Several years ago, we visited Jeanette's daughter's home for Thanksgiving. It was a joyous occasion as we all gathered together for our Thanksgiving celebration, which Susan and Jeff hold outdoors regardless of the weather. Jeanette's grandson Colin had just landed a new job after graduating from college, and he came to the celebration. He had just purchased a new iPhone and spent the greater part of the day nervously checking his e-mail and looking things up on his new phone. On several occasions, he called our attention to some of its features. At the end of the day, his father said, "Is that all you are going to do today?" Colin's body attended the Thanksgiving celebration, but his mind had been taken prisoner by this marvelous new device. My second example is from my own family: my grandson, who had come to our home for Christmas dinner one year. He had just received some new electronic games (from his parents and grandparents) for his Wii computer and spent most of the afternoon with his body draped over the seat of our stuffed chair, and his knees on the floor. After my son and his family left, Jeanette wondered if Mikey was sick, because he hadn't said much. I said, "No, he was just playing games on his Wii." And I am sure that your family is not much different from ours.

These machines have the power to take total control of the minds of our children as well as to drain the pocketbooks of their parents at the same time. It is as if our children and youth are worshipping these machines, hoping that the machine will tell them something that they are desperately looking for or to provide them with answers to questions they can't seem to answer for themselves. And these machines are extracting a terrible toll on our society. Texting while driving is a major problem, and although it is illegal in New York State, it still is regularly practiced, with deadly results. (Five female high school graduates recently died in a head-on crash near Bloomfield, New York, because the driver was texting to another car of girls, lost control of the car, and drove head-on into an oncoming truck.)

I could write down many other examples, but you get my point: *we are becoming slaves to these gods!* We worship them because they are smarter than we are, they are faster, and they take us to places that we can't physically go, or introduce us to people and things we would normally never have met or experienced in a lifetime. And they are robbing us of the experience of being human. Haven't we been warned about these gods before? Do you remember the Ten Commandments that were given to us several thousand years ago in the Bible (Exodus 20:2–17)? "Thou shalt have no other gods before me." "Thou shalt not make unto thee any graven image, or any likeness of anything that is in heaven above, or that is in the earth beneath, or that is in the water under the earth." As a part of my Christian upbringing, I had to memorize the Ten Commandments. It is forbidden to teach them in our public schools today. Even our churches have chosen to ignore these basic fundamental moral rules of living. Our parents, teachers, and preachers have been convinced that one should never say no to our children. In terms of today's thinking, one should not draw any lines in the sand, or boundaries that should not be crossed for fear that we might stunt a child's ability to think or explore outside of these boxes. Let me list here the Ten Commandments that were given to us in the Bible so you will not need to look them up for yourself:

1. Thou shalt have no other gods before me.

2. Thou shalt not make unto thee any graven image, or any likeness of any thing that is in heaven, or that is in the earth beneath, or that is in the water under the earth. Thou shalt not bow down thyself to them, nor serve them.

3. Thou shalt not take the name of the Lord thy God in vain.

4. Remember the Sabbath day, to keep it holy.

5. Honor thy father and thy mother: that thy days may be long upon the land which the Lord thy God giveth thee.

6. Thou shalt not kill.

7. Thou shalt not commit adultery.

8. Thou shalt not steal.

9. Thou shalt not bear false witness against a neighbor.

10. Thou shalt not covet thy neighbor's house, thou shalt not covet thy neighbor's wife, nor his manservant, not his maidservant, nor his ox, nor his ass, nor anything that is thy neighbor's.

When I was young, I did not understand the second commandment very well, because all I could ever associate with this verse was an image of a golden calf, which the Israelites were worshipping at the time the commandments were given. Having grown up on a farm, I could relate to calves, but they were not of the "golden idol" variety. No, our calves had to be fed and cared for like any other animal. We cared for them and their well-being, because our living depended upon it, but surely we did not worship them! But now I can see clearly that we have created many different kinds of idols for ourselves and that we are actively worshipping them each today. And the list doesn't contain just computers, smartphones, televisions, video games, the Internet, or other electronic devices. One can add to this list our professional athletes, our superstar entertainers, sex, drugs, money, power—and the list just keeps growing longer and longer.

We try to have it both ways. We want our freedom to do as we please and to pursue life, liberty, and happiness without having any rules to follow. *But it's not working very well for us.* And after all of man's inventions that relieve us from doing any real physical work or any kind of mental exercises (thinking, planning, creating), our lives seem to be more and more controlled by these machines and devices that we have created. *Instead of being freed, we are becoming more like slaves to these gods!*

12

MAKING SENSE OUT OF THE LAST HUNDRED YEARS

ACCORDING TO TOFFLER, the agricultural wave of civilization began around 8000 BC and the industrial wave began around AD 1650. But the number of changes that people today have to face seems to me to be unprecedented compared with all the changes and challenges that humans have faced since the dawn of civilization. And in the last twenty years, *a tsunami wave of disruptions has completely turned our society upside down both economically and socially!*

Many people have asked me, "Why has there been so much change?" In the early 1900s, 41 percent of the workforce living in the United States was still directly involved in agriculture. By year 2000, only 2 percent of the workforce is employed in agriculture. The steepest part of the decline in the agricultural workforce occurred in the forties, fifties, and sixties - during my school years. The industrial society in the United States was tremendously accelerated by World War I and World War II as the technologies that were developed for these wars started filtering into general society. One example is the invention of radar which was used to track ships and airplanes; radar was the forerunner of television. Another example is the invention of the atomic bomb; now we use atomic energy to generate electricity. A third invention was the use of the V2 rocket by the Germans during WWII; now, we use rockets to launch our communications satellites and to explore the vast space around the earth and beyond. I grew up in the fifties and sixties, which according to my high school teacher Harold Taylor was the "sweet spot" of the last seventy-five years. The men returning from the war were eager to begin earning a living and raising a family. Television had just come onto the scene, but the TV was a source of news, weather, and entertainment, and it had not yet become the treacherous device that it is today. The machines that had been used to turn out the guns, tanks, and airplanes during the Second World War were now being used to create some of the most beautiful cars that Detroit has ever produced: classics such as the 1955 Chevrolet Bel-Air, the 1955 Ford Thunderbird, and the 1955 Mercury Monterey. It was a time when drugs were not even known in the little rural community that I grew up in, and the township where my school was located was "dry"—bars and beer joints were prohibited. Young people gathered at the local drive-in for a hamburger and a glass of root beer—if they had any extra money in their pockets!

But all the idealism of the fifties and sixties began to fade after the Korean War and the Vietnam War. Along came the widespread use of digital calculators in the early seventies and the introduction of the personal computer in 1981, which suddenly changed everything: we started down a path that freed our minds from having to think and memorize things, because we were able to look up the answer on a computer.

In the midfifties, only 10 percent of our US workforce was still engaged in agriculture; that number has dwindled to less than 2 percent today. (Extrapolation of the data presented in the USDA report, "The 20th Century Transformation of U.S. Agriculture and Farm Policy.) Also in the fifties, the number of people working in service jobs started to outnumber the number of people directly involved in manufacturing (in 1950, 26.4% of the labor force was involved in manufacturing; 27.3 per cent of the labor force was clerical, sales, service. Source: "Labor Force for Historical Statistics of the United States, Millennial Edition," Susan B. Carter.

How many of you remember your mothers or fathers or family members working on the farm or in a factory assembling cars, clothes, or shoes, or as an elevator or telephone operator, or pumping gas at the local service station, or working as secretaries or bank tellers? Most of these jobs have been replaced by machines that not only do their work without pay but have eliminated much of the human thinking that went along with them. And the machines that we have created are growing not only in strength but also in speed, since their brains (microprocessors) are based upon semiconductors that double their processing speed every year!

We humans are finding ourselves on a treadmill that forces us to keep up the pace that has been set by the machines. But that is obviously a losing battle. Humans need to rest eight hours a day and they need time to exercise their bodies, socialize with other humans, and above all to dream. Our political system is in turmoil as our politicians struggle with increasing the minimum wage, increasing welfare benefits, or trying to find a way to redistribute wealth based upon some system that is not rooted in wages. And while all of this is going on, our education system is only turning out more of the same kind of individuals who will not be able to find a job based upon their liberal arts degrees. Even our top engineers won't find work here in the United States, because they now have to compete globally for engineering work.

We humans seem to have a major flaw built into us. We are never satisfied with what we have been given or the hands that have been dealt to us. The writers of Genesis 2 and 3 in the Bible recognized this fault as they described the Garden of Eden, where Adam and Eve lived. Adam and Eve had it made. They had each other for company, they had all the fruit they could eat from the garden, they did not have to do any work, and they didn't have to worry about keeping a wardrobe full of the latest clothes! But they did have one restriction: they were told not to eat of the fruit from the Tree of the Knowledge of Good and Evil. Well, they just weren't satisfied, and they broke the only rule that had been given to them. As a result, they were cast out of the garden, condemned to live a life filled with all the human ailments, trials, and tribulations that we experience. Their miserable lives ended in death.

13

WHAT WILL THE NEXT FIFTY YEARS BRING?

THE FACT THAT we can recognize a problem and write down the problem so that the problem can be communicated to others often goes a long way toward solving it. Our hope (and our curse) is embedded in the sentence "We (humans) are never satisfied with what we have been given or the hand that has been dealt to us." And although I can offer no instant solutions to all of society's problems that have been created by our own technological advances, I do have enough confidence in our own ability to teach the machines who is boss and to make sure that we (humans) are in control and are the benefactors of their labor and our ability to think!

Our society needs to return to the fundamental rules that were given to us more than two thousand years ago. Yes, it would mean giving up some of our "freedoms" to live a life that has no boundaries, but in doing so, it would save most of us a lot of misery and grief.

I can cite many examples of humans obtaining all that could be possibly desired by man but still not being satisfied. One example is Tiger

Woods. He had it all: a beautiful wife, children, fame, wealth, and the distinction of being the world's greatest golfer. But still he was not satisfied, and he chose to break one of the commandments that were given to us: thou shalt not commit adultery. His world came crashing down around him. I am sure that he perfectly remembered the rules of golf that his father taught him when he was a little boy. But somewhere in his professional career, he "crossed the line" of the moral rules that have been given to all of us. In the process he lost his family, much of his wealth, and the respect of those who followed his golfing career.

I can foresee medical science advancing to the point where our machines will decide if you or I will be born or if our life will be prolonged or not when we grow old. A technician will draw a bit of embryonic fluid from the womb, and a machine will analyze the fluid to see if certain parameters are met. If those parameters are not met, you will not be born! That will be just the first in a series of decisions where machines will control most phases of human life. The problem with this matter-of-fact kind of approach to life is that machines have no morals; they only do what has been programmed into their computers!

I am not a futurist. I have trouble predicting what will happen to me tomorrow, let alone what our world will look like fifty years from now. But it does seem clear to me that humans will be living under some kind of centrally controlled knowledge system. Each generation will no longer need to go back and relearn all the things that you and I had to learn by experience. And it will be this central knowledge system that makes most of the major decisions for us. I doubt that this knowledge-based system will be morals based. Yes, it will be a knowledge-based system generated by humans, but the answers to the human struggle will be based upon other considerations such as financial requirements, available resources, or perhaps by some special interest group or political party. The question then becomes "Who or what will be the great benefactor from the implementation of such a central knowledge-based system?" For example, the human race might be the benefactor if the knowledge-based system implemented sweeping worldwide changes to reverse the effects of global warming or if the knowledge-based system detected an impending Earth collision with a large asteroid and responded by destroying the asteroid before it destroyed the Earth. Or the human race might be the winner if the knowledge-based system implemented some kind of worldwide population control based upon, let's say, sustainable natural resources. But clearly the future of the human race could easily become one of slavery, with every aspect of human life being controlled by the knowledge-based system. Which one will it be?

Man has already tasted of the fruit from the Tree of the
Knowledge of Good and Evil.
He can think, invent, and solve problems,
But he can't save himself!

Made in the USA
Charleston, SC
26 March 2015